DOWNSIDE ABBEY

An Architectural History

✠ DOWNSIDE ABBEY

An Architectural History

Edited by Dom Aidan Bellenger

MERRELL
LONDON • NEW YORK

Preface

The Abbey of St Gregory the Great at Downside is a community of monks of the English Benedictine Congregation. Its beautiful abbey church, one of the great masterpieces of the Gothic Revival, is the subject of this book. The monks of St Gregory's, in the twenty-first century, attempt to live a rule of life that was compiled in the sixth century by St Benedict, in whose interpretation of the Christian life prayer was at the centre of all things.

The Rule of St Benedict contains no architectural instructions, but its emphasis on self-sufficiency and enclosure was crucial to the shaping and contextualizing of the monastic ideal. In the fifty-second chapter ('Of the Oratory of the Monastery'), St Benedict underlines the special character of the place of prayer in the Benedictine complex:

> Let the oratory be what its name implies, and let nothing else be done or kept there. When the Work of God is finished, let all go out in deep silence, and let reverence for God be observed, so that any brother who may wish to pray privately be not hindered by another's misbehaviour. And at other times also, if anyone wish to pray secretly, let him just go in and pray: not in a loud voice, but with tears and fervour of heart. He, therefore, who does not behave so, shall not be permitted to remain in the oratory when the Work of God is ended, lest he should, as we have said, be a hindrance to another.

St Gregory the Great tells us in his life of St Benedict that in the foundation of the monastery of Terracina, in the province of Rome, St Benedict told his disciples he was sending instructions on the buildings; but the earliest surviving monastic plan is that of St Gall in Switzerland, which dates from *c.* AD 820. The association of Benedictine monks with both the Romanesque (through the dominance of the great French abbey of Cluny) and the Gothic styles (through the patronage of Abbot Suger of St-Denis) meant that they never became tied to one architectural form, as did the Jesuits in their prime. Indeed, many of Europe's most historic monasteries happily adapted the exuberance of Baroque during the Counter-Reformation. Monasteries, often seen as thresholds of Heaven, looked for enlightenment both spiritual and architectural, and Downside, deeply influenced by the Gothic Revival of the nineteenth century, is suffused with light.

Downside's monastic identity is part of the nineteenth-century European rediscovery of Benedictine ideals, but its inspiration is predominantly English. A Benedictine monk takes a vow of 'stability of place', which roots him in one community for life, and Benedictine places take on a characteristic sense of order and permanence. Downside, while reacting to change, has become deeply rooted in the Somerset countryside. Many different building materials have been used in the church's construction, especially in its pavement and side altars, but the core of the structure (revealed clearly in the austere, 'temporary' west front) is locally quarried lias stone. The limestone oolite used on the elevations both inside and outside is Doulting ashlar, which associates the building not only with the local land but also with the nearby great medieval churches of Glastonbury and Wells.

Downside Abbey is the physical heart of a large family made up of the monastic community, school, parishes and all those who form part of the abbey's workforce. It is, above all else, a place of prayer and silence, an affirmation in stone of the abiding presence of God in His world, and an incarnational statement of the Benedictine aphorism that 'God be glorified in all things'.

Dom Aidan Bellenger
Twelfth Abbot of Downside

Downside Abbey and School
Schematic Plan

1	Old House *c.* 1700
2	Henry Edmund Goodridge 1823
3	Charles Hansom 1854
4	Dunn and Hansom 1873–1882
5	Thomas Garner 1905
6	Leonard Stokes 1911
7	Frederick Walters 1915
8	Sir Giles Gilbert Scott 1925–39
9	Brett, Boyd and Bosanquet 1957–61
10	Francis Pollen 1962–70
11	NVB Architects 2006–2007

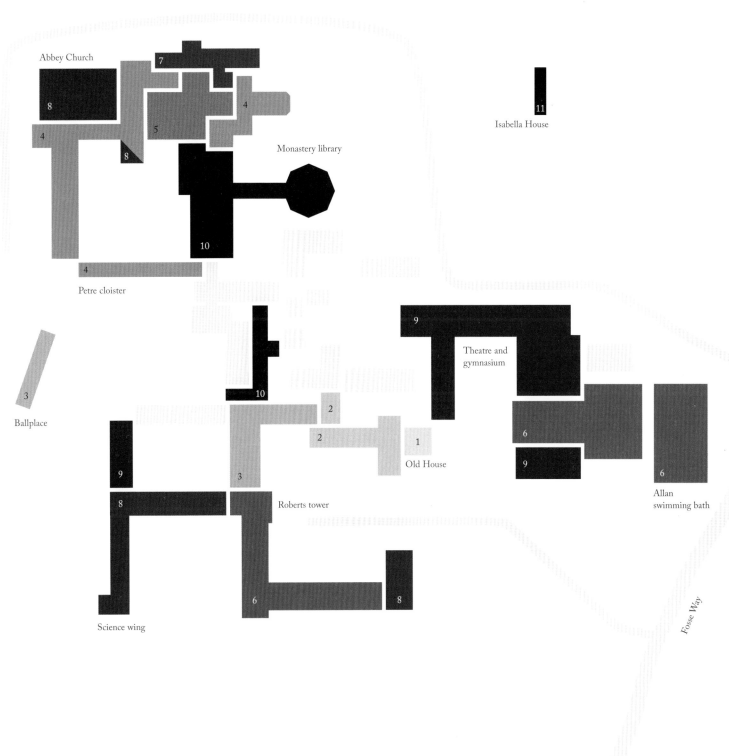

N

Abbey Church

8

4

7

5

8

4

Monastery library

4

10

Petre cloister

11

Isabella House

9

Theatre and
gymnasium

3

Ballplace

10

2

2

1

6

Old House

9

6

3

Allan
swimming bath

9

8

Roberts tower

8

6

8

Science wing

100 ft

20 m

Fosse Way

Models of Monasticism:
The Churches and Chapels
of St Gregory's, Downside

Dom Aidan Bellenger

The buildings of St Gregory's Abbey and School at Downside form an impressive group, what Nikolaus Pevsner calls 'Pugin's dream of the future of English Catholicism at last come true'. They are dominated by the 'commanding' tower, nearly 166 feet (51 m) high, which draws attention to the church, the most splendid part of the ensemble.[1] What follows here is not intended to provide a detailed architectural description or a history of the present fabric; that is contained in subsequent chapters. It is intended, rather, to suggest that these buildings, and their predecessors, stand for a developing modern view of the revived monastic life.

The 'black monk' community of St Gregory (of the English Benedictine Congregation), which eventually settled at Downside, now in the parish of Stratton-on-the-Fosse in Somerset, on the Fosse Way 12 miles (19 km) south of Bath, was first established at Douai in Flanders, a university and manufacturing town that had developed into a centre for English

Catholic exiles during the Elizabethan period. A college for the training of the secular clergy, the English College, had been founded by Cardinal William Allen in 1568. Between 1605 and 1607 a group of English and Welsh monks from various Continental monasteries gathered in the town, where they obtained the support and patronage of Philip de Caverel, abbot of St Vedast's monastery at Arras, France, in their endeavour to establish an exiled – but English – monastic house.[2]

The Douai community was not a large one (twenty-four monks was the average number in residence[3]) and it shared its home with monks of St Vedast studying at the town's university. Nevertheless, although lacking distinction, the buildings of the monastery were spacious and urbane. 'The general effect', as David Lunn, a recent historian of the English Benedictines, has put it, 'was impressive: the Gothic chapel, with its lofty windows and lantern, and the slim and elegant college

The monastery building nestles under the abbey tower. The spiral staircase, as seen in the smaller tower on the left, is a much-repeated feature of the built landscape at Downside.

buildings, four storeys high'.[4] Within the church, the monks, in line with Abbot Caverel's instructions, celebrated the liturgy with great solemnity. They had 'heavy choir duties', compensated in a traditionally Benedictine way with 'good food'.[5]

The whole establishment, despite the markedly Spanish character of its customs (reflecting the original Iberian houses of some of the brethren, as well as Caverel's taste), was self-consciously English.[6] Its buildings were the headquarters of a community the principal apostolic function of which was, through prayer and action, 'the conversion of their native land, for which they dedicated themselves at their profession by a missionary oath'.[7] Much was made of the shadowy figure of Dom Sigebert Buckley, monk of Mary Tudor's Westminster Abbey, and his link with the early days of the re-established English Congregation.[8] The foundation stone of the monastery church was laid in 1614 and the building was dedicated, significantly, on the feast of St Augustine of England.[9]

The church was a spacious aisled building, a hall church in the Gothic taste with an eastern apse and a compact choir. Its inspiration and construction were local, similar to the church Caverel had erected for the Jesuits at Arras, and owed little or nothing to English models. Recusant memory expressed itself verbally rather than visually, as did European monasticism in general. Baroque, in its local varieties, became as normative for the Benedictines of the seventeenth and eighteenth centuries as it was for the Counter-Reformation Congregation. The grandest of the Continental English Benedictine monasteries was the abbey of Lamspringe in the vicinity of Hildesheim, now in Germany. Its church had a grand baroque interior with a simple, if monumental, exterior, and again was designed and built by local hands. The only hint at its English connections was its iconography: stained glass and statuary were inspired by the English saints, and its crypt enshrined the relics of St Oliver Plunkett.

The overall character of the church at Douai can be glimpsed in the model of the town made in 1709 and kept in the Douai museum. The town's Municipal Archives preserve drawings of the chapel by A. Robaut, as well as a plan. It remained intact during the late eighteenth-century rebuilding of the monastic and collegiate buildings (which exist, in part, today), and survived the French Revolution. The school buildings, begun in 1770 during the priorship of Dom Augustine Moore, were on an ambitious scale. The original church was demolished in 1833, and in 1840 a new chapel, designed by A.W.N. Pugin (1812–1852), was started for the English Benedictine monks of St Edmund's, Paris, who moved into the site. The fittings of the original church, with the exception of a few paintings and the evocative grave marker of Dom Rudesind Barlow, the second prior, were subject to change over the almost two centuries of their life, and are now lost. The antiquary William Cole, paying a visit in 1765, found that the former high altar had been dismantled and replaced by 'an ordinary extemporary one [placed] in the middle of the church'. The monks' choir stalls had been moved right up against the east wall, and the monk who showed him round said that the arrangement was not merely a makeshift during reconstruction of the church: it was permanent and represented a concession to a 'Taste and Fashion … now very prevalent in France' for increasing congregational participation in services.[10] Fashions in church furnishing always have their precedents.

The monastic church, as later at Downside, doubled as a chapel for the students in the school established alongside, a foundation that catered for the education both of future monks and of lay students. The latter provided not only an income for the community but also a well-disposed support group for the monks on the mission.

The life of the Douai community came to an abrupt end in 1794, when the monks were forced to leave the Continent after Revolutionary France

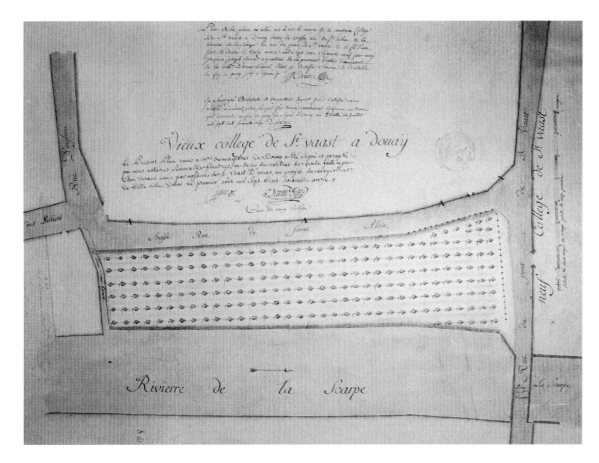

LEFT, TOP
Location plan of the 'Old College of St Vaast at Douay', dated 1771. St Gregory's, Douai, was founded in the early seventeenth century by Philip de Caverel, abbot of St Vedast's at Arras.

LEFT, BOTTOM
The 'slim and elegant' buildings of the English College at Douai, with chapel to the right.

declared war on England. On its arrival in England the community was housed, through the courtesy of the Smythe family, in the specially converted Acton Burnell Hall in Shropshire. The chapel for the monks' use, completed in 1799, was a typical Catholic gentry construction: externally severe, internally fussy:

> It did not have the Baroque glory of Wardour [Castle, in Wiltshire], but the walls were blue, the ceiling and cornice white, the capitals of the simple pillars were gilded, daubings of light angels, 'more heads with a pair of wings', floated on the wall around the altar, below them gilded flowers on a dark violet background; the benches, pews and choir were painted in imitation oak, while, to vary matters still further, the doors, pulpit and organ were painted in imitation mahogany; the altar was draped with two velvet curtains of crimson with gold fringe and tassels – but these curtains too were only painted representations.[11]

The pastiche chapel, which survives in an altered, secularized and much less flamboyant form,[12] was what it appeared to be – the private chapel of a prosperous Catholic family adjusted, for the time being, to the needs of a small religious community. The monks were at Acton Burnell for reasons of charity and of expediency, and although efforts were made to carry out ceremonies 'as much as possible as they were at Douay', the monastery at Acton Burnell was a stopgap community.[13] Its buildings – country house and small chapel – represented its plight: re-exiled monasticism dedicated to the English mission and to education (the school, much diminished, continued) but without a true home, and perhaps, lacking real stability, without a future.

The buildings acquired at Downside, a sizable plain house of the late seventeenth century and adjoining properties, were in a then remote part of the country, on a high spot 600 feet (180 m) above sea level, in an area dedicated to coal-mining and agriculture. The first chapel for monastery and school was a utilitarian ground-floor room in what is now known as the 'Old House'. It was soon replaced (in 1823) by an extraordinary construction by H.E. Goodridge (1797–1864), externally rather like the nave and transepts of a large Gothic church, but in reality a miniature monastery and school; only the upper part of the transept formed the chapel. This Gothic essay, described by Pugin as 'good, for its date', with its somewhat faint echoes of the cathedrals of Salisbury and Wells, represented a substantial statement of faith by the community: the monks were here to stay.[14] Goodridge's design was chosen in preference to others at least partly because it was in 'our national style'.[15] Its character was solidly collegiate rather than monastic.

The early years at Downside were dominated by conflict with Dom Augustine Baines and his new college at Prior Park in Bath. Between the Gothic of Downside and the Classicism of Prior Park there was something of a 'style war'. A contemporary example of such a conflict occurred in Wigan in Lancashire, where in 1818 two Catholic chapels were built on the same street, one Jesuit (and Classical), the other secular (and Gothic). The English Benedictines themselves, at the time Goodridge's chapel was commissioned, were still predominantly Classics rather than Goths.

The 'Old Chapel' at Downside, acting as both priory and parish church, epitomized a new approach to monasticism, attempting with its Gothic atmosphere to recapture the still-elusive spirit of medieval monasticism and to bring monasticism into the open. Until the Victorian period, however, it was an antiquarian rather than an archaeological approach. Gowns, more academic than clerical, were worn until the reintroduction of the full habit in the 1840s.[16] The Divine Office was sung not to plainsong but to polyphony, with a variety if not a quality appropriate

A quiet country monastery. Old House and Old Chapel stand together, Classical and Gothic, in rural seclusion.

to an opera house, under the direction of an Italian Count (Joseph Mazzinghi) playing an organ imported from the Royal Pavilion in Brighton. The monastery and its school were small in scale and limited in aspiration;[17] as at Douai, the original monastery at Downside was the 'feed' of a dispersed mission.[18] The 'permanent' community was small and youthful.[19]

The abbey church as it now stands, complete except for its west front (for which various plans have been made), is the product – and sign – of the renewal of monastic life, in its fullness, in the last hundred years. Downside retained (and retains) some of its parishes, but concentrated its work on its resident community; the school developed into 'a leading public school'; the community (which included Cardinal Aidan Gasquet, Abbot Cuthbert Butler and Dom David Knowles) developed a reputation for learning as an Edwardian Athens of English Catholicism; and the monastic liturgy was celebrated with especial splendour.[20] 'Observance' became the watchword.

The church was not built all at once, but developed in the medieval manner, under the direction of successive architects.[21] Some drawings made by Pugin for Downside are preserved. The design of 1839, perhaps 'the first "correct" setting for monastic life in England since the dissolution', shows Pugin, a twenty-seven-year-old convert, far ahead of his fellow Catholics in his understanding of how a building might express visually 'a particular ethos of life, in this case the Benedictine Rule'.[22] The plans were dominated by the proposals for a great monastic church, complete with a central spire, western towers and a ten-bay nave. Nothing materialized, and, in common with many buildings at Downside, it remained a dream. But such dreams were important. They revealed the ambitions and aspirations of the community, and were to lead at the end of the nineteenth century to the beginnings of the present abbey church.

A proposal of 1846, in the Pugin manner, by Charles Hansom (1817–1888) led to the construction of some picturesque school buildings, but it was not until the 1870s that a plan by Hansom's son Edward (1842–1900) and Archibald M. Dunn (1832–1917) to build a completely new monastery – again, like Pugin's, with a dominant abbey church – was implemented. Of this the chief memorial is the transept, completed in 1882.[23] This represents that stage of the Gothic Revival that attempted to marry 'the Gothic' (the 'English' style) with the demands of an increasingly 'Roman' hierarchy. The result is rather overwhelming; decoration is heavily applied with 'an almost Spanish effusiveness'.[24] In Peter Anson's opinion, Dunn and Hansom's work was 'a perfect expression of Catholic taste during the 'eighties and early 'nineties'.[25] This part of the building dates from a time of great internal controversy in the community: a time that decided whether the community was to be missionary or monastic;[26] a time, too, when Gasquet abolished the 'old' English pronunciation of Church Latin and 'introduced the Italian on the plea of conformity with the practice of other communities'.[27]

Dunn and Hansom's buildings – which include the Lady chapel (1888) and other chapels around the choir (by 1890) – were left incomplete. The Lady chapel, decorated by Ninian Comper (1864–1960), had as its centrepiece 'one of the first unchallenged acceptances of "the English Altar"'.[28] In its quality and finish, the chapel also prefigured the monastic choir, by Thomas Garner (1839–1906). This is an essay in the grand manner, symbolizing a religious community that had come of age. Its scale and details are of great splendour and prayerfulness, 'the expression', as Dom Augustine James put it, 'of a religious spirit which will remain'.[29] In Shane Leslie's words, it seemed 'as though Glastonbury were restored, rebuilt for England'.[30]

There was a very real sense of the continuity between Downside and its medieval antecedents. The high altar was built from stone taken from the ruins of Glastonbury Abbey, as was the altar in the chapel of St Sylvia, crowned by a medieval *mensa* from the

Giles Gilbert Scott's soaring
and beautifully constructed
nave suffused with natural
light embodies the aspirations
and self-confidence of
the monastery.

formerly monastic church at Cannington in north Somerset. There were echoes of St Albans Cathedral in the building. The arms of Glastonbury and St Albans are on the jambs of the arch at the east end of the sacristy, above the principal vesting bench.

The church is both a repository of a number of important relics and the resting place of some significant figures in the local history of the Catholic Church. The relic of the True Cross in its seventeenth-century reliquary, perhaps once in Westminster Abbey, and the head of St Thomas of Hereford link Downside with the pre-Reformation Church. The body of St Oliver Plunkett (his head is preserved at Drogheda, Co. Louth) and relics of English martyrs link the community to the heroic days of its revival. The tombs of many of the Vicars Apostolic of the Western District (including Bishop Baines) show the continuity of the church with the Recusant Church. The tombs of Bishop Morris and Cardinal Gasquet and of Abbots Ford and Ramsay proclaim the building's place in the self-confident nineteenth- and twentieth-century Catholic Church.

The use of works of art to complement the architectural detail also stressed the continuity of the church building with the lost world of English medieval monasticism. The gifts of old master paintings, including some Flemish 'primitives', linked the church stylistically with the fifteenth and early sixteenth centuries and provided appropriate altarpieces. The most evocative work of art is probably the fine Madonna and Child in dark wood, dating from the 1460s and presented by Cardinal Gasquet, which stands in the south aisle. Contemporary with it may be the seated figure of St Peter at the far end of the south aisle, but that is less fine in quality and is damaged.

Among the vestments in the sacristy is a small but important collection of late medieval embroideries, including the Glover chasuble, with its characteristic 'glove' motif, and the Bordesley chasuble, a rare link with a medieval monastic abbey (Bordesley,

a Cistercian foundation in the Midlands). The vestments also include many designed and executed at Downside itself in the middle years of the twentieth century. The plate, too, encompasses medieval and modern. A fifteenth-century Spanish processional cross is a highlight of the earlier period, and the massive Von Hügel monstrance, an architectural work in itself nearly 3 feet (1 m) high, is perhaps the most spectacular piece. It was designed by J.A. Pippet and made in 1900 by Hardman, Powell & Company, and includes 1827 diamonds with many other precious stones.

The architecture of the church and the high quality of its furnishings are intended not as a visual feast but as an enhancement of the liturgy. The daily conventual Mass, the annual Holy Week ceremonies with the Easter Vigil at their core, the occasional monastic professions and ordinations, the abbatial blessings and, once in a church's existence (in 1935 at Downside), the service of dedication and consecration give life to the space.

The choir stalls were designed by Giles Gilbert Scott after consultation with the drawings of Dom Ephrem Seddon (an architect monk of Downside, advised by F.H. Crossley, the authority on English medieval woodwork), and executed by Ferdinand Stüflesser at Ortisei, in what was then the Austrian Tyrol, in Austrian oak. Installed in 1932, and gradually augmented, they were moved to their present position when the sanctuary was remodelled by Francis Pollen (see p. 215). They provide the central setting of the abbey's worship.

At Downside, the monastic round is augmented during term time by the school. The abbey church in its role as school chapel has few peers; apart from the great chapel at Lancing College in West Sussex, only those schools attached to a cathedral can really compete. The great choir organ unites the liturgy of abbey and school. The organ in the south transept is concealed by a grand screen erected in 1931 to a design by Sir Giles Gilbert Scott and executed by Stüflesser.

The Madonna and Child, a late Gothic masterwork, at home in its revived Gothic setting.

OPPOSITE
The late Gothic Spanish
processional cross is an
exuberant symbol of the
cosmopolitanism of the
abbey church.

RIGHT
The Von Hügel monstrance,
a Victorian memorial to
devotion and prosperity, is
resplendent with a galaxy
of precious stones.

OPPOSITE
The choir stalls – the monks'
place of worship, where
the daily work of God is
celebrated – form a quiet,
enclosed space at the heart
of the building.

LEFT
The south transept, showing
a completed sector of the
Dunn and Hansom building
and the top of the organ.

The single bell of the abbey church, 'Great Bede', was drawn by horses to Downside from Chilcompton station in 1903. It was cast by Taylor of Loughborough, was 5 feet 4½ inches (1.64 m) high and 6 feet 10½ inches (2.1 m) wide at its mouth, and cost £721 2s. 9d. The inscription on its headstock, '*Ego sum Rogerius Beda Vaughan, Archiepiscopus Sydniensis 1877–1883*', is accompanied by the acrostic '*Voco Alumnos Ut Gratias Hodie Agant Numini*' ('I call all living here to render thanks this day to God').

The instrument itself, which was installed the same year, is a four-manual electronic Compton organ, an exemplary instrument for its period (see pp. 173–75).

The tower contains the abbey's single bell, 'Great Bede', blessed on 15 June 1903, a memorial to Archbishop Vaughan of Sydney. Cast by Taylor of Loughborough, with its total weight of seven tons it was (on its first ring) the ninth heaviest bell in England.

The Old Chapel served at first as the place of worship for local Catholics, but as the monastic and scholastic identity of the main buildings became refined, a separate parish chapel was built on the Fosse Way in the village of Stratton-on-the-Fosse. St Benedict's Church (see pp. 28–29) reflected the developments more amply demonstrated in the abbey, echoing with its churchyard and tower (with bells) a medieval village church. The present structure began life as a school but was transformed by Charles Hansom into a church, which opened in 1857. Extended in 1913, the church was transformed internally by Dom Ethelbert Horne, parish priest for almost half a century. In 1915 a magnificent decorated rood screen

and reredos, designed by Seddon and made by William Chivers, a local craftsman, was installed. Dom Gregory Murray, a man of very fixed opinions, in 'the spirit of Vatican II' removed most of Horne's screen as early as 1957, using the Bath architect Martin Fisher; in the 1960s Murray introduced a stone free-standing altar, now suitably concealed (with the reform of the reform) behind frontals. Part of the screen serves as an organ loft.

At Downside, the school buildings form a separate unit, but the abbey church and the monastic buildings are fully integrated. The north cloister runs alongside the south aisle of the abbey church and has gallery chapels above it. The main monastery building, externally rather like a railway hotel or minor country house, has within it a twelve-bay cloister, the 'West Cloister', some 161 feet (49 m) in length, 14 feet (4.3 m) in breadth and the same height, of great magnificence. It is built in Bath stone with lines of dark Ham Hill stone in its groined vault, and has a stone staircase at the southern end and a wooden one at the northern. The ground floor of the monastery, which contains the public rooms,

RIGHT, TOP
The exterior of St Benedict's, Stratton-on-the-Fosse, a Somerset Catholic parish church complementing its monastic neighbour.

RIGHT, BOTTOM
Dom Ethelbert Horne inherited the church with a basic screen. This photograph shows the church in its glory, after his transformations, with rood screen crowned by ostrich-egg reliquaries, and altar with riddle posts.

OPPOSITE
The rood, without attendant figures, and the reredos, made in Italy but depicting local Saints, survived the simplification of Dom Gregory Murray; so did the statue of St Vigor, patron of Stratton's medieval parish church.

In the east cloister, which links the principal public rooms of the monastery to the nave of the abbey church, the work of Dunn and Hansom blends into that of Giles Gilbert Scott. Abbot Ramsay's tomb is prominent in the north wall of the nave.

The stone staircase of the monastery shows Dunn and Hansom at their most baronial. It leads up from the Petre cloister to the monastic cells on the first floor.

including a chapter room with a fine fireplace, gives on to the cloister.

A number of the ground-floor rooms were originally set aside for the library, but only as a temporary expedient, and plans for a purpose-built monastic library formed part of all the major proposals for the completion of the buildings. The library as built by Pollen in 1965–70, to the southeast of the abbey church, is in a modern idiom, but is set where it could easily be mistaken for a chapter house in the round, such as the one at nearby Wells Cathedral. It can be compared with its contemporary, Mount Angel Abbey Library, built at St Benedict, Oregon, by the great Finnish architect Alvar Aalto, which is lit in a similar, lantern-like way.

The abbey church was completed in its present form by Scott. The nave, of 1923–25, is starker and lighter than the east end, and the tower – 'thoroughly Somerset in its feeling' and finished in 1938 as an appropriate memorial to Cardinal Gasquet – crowns the building and gives it distinction from a distance.[31]

The building of the church was funded by individual benefactors and by the monastic community itself. The numerous side chapels, akin to medieval chantries, encouraged family identification with a particular space. The nave (and the refitting of the Lady chapel) was a memorial to Downside pupils who died in the First World War. The chapel of the Sacred Heart, with its ceramic panels by Adam Kossowski, was completed in 1954. The variety of style and the subtlety of much of the decoration of the chapels reflect the collaborative input of the monastic community.

Until 1899 the English Benedictines were a centralized congregation with a President General, who was elected for four years by the General Chapter of the monks and assisted by his council or regimen. After 1899 the individual monasteries, previously priories, were elevated to abbatial status and their ordinary government placed in the hands of the abbots. The solemnly professed monks of the community, the chapter and the abbot's council provided advice and consent, especially on such important matters as the development of the Church. Individual members of the chapter played a disproportionate role in influencing the Church's growth, either through knowledge or through persistence. In the nineteenth century Dom Gilbert Dolan consistently argued for an abbey church on the scale of the great medieval monasteries, and backed up the initiatives of Priors Murphy and Gasquet. Dom Anselm Rutherford – an enthusiastic champion of Scott – took a great interest in the furnishings and fabrics of the church, and, while working at St John's, Bath (then a Downside dependency), employed Scott to design the striking basilican church of St Alphege in Bath's Oldfield Park.[32] The involvement of monks, architects and craftsmen, of clerks of works and bursars (the monks responsible for the material aspects of the monastery's life), are all faithfully recorded by James in *The Story of Downside Abbey Church*.[33]

The visual impact of Downside Abbey Church is stunning, and, whatever its relationship to medieval precedents, it has a unique nineteenth- and twentieth-century character. Gothic Revivalism was, perhaps, the medium Catholicism employed to distance itself from its contemporary world – a form of inverted modernism. Downside has about it something of the character of the church reconstructions by the great etcher F.L. Griggs, known to many in the community. In his *Anglia Perdita* of *c*. 1921, for example, Griggs imagined a building at the last moment before the dissolution of the monasteries. Downside, by contrast, showed the possibility of revival and monasticism reborn. It is not only a building but also the setting for a living community and a complete model of a developed monastic view.

1. N. Pevsner, *North Somerset and Bristol*, London and Harmondsworth (Penguin) 1973, p. 183.
2. H. Connolly, *Some Dates and Documents for the Early History of Our House*, Stratton-on-the-Fosse, Somerset (Downside Abbey) 1930, *passim*.
3. D. Lunn, *The English Benedictines, 1540–1688*, London (Burns & Oates) 1980, p. 174.
4. *Ibid.*, p. 173.
5. *Ibid.*, p. 182.
6. *Ibid.*
7. L. Almond (ed.), *Downside Abbey and School, 1814–1914*, Exeter (Paternoster Press) 1914, p. xi.
8. J. McCann and C. Cary-Elwes, *Ampleforth and its Origins*, London (Burns, Oates & Washbourne) 1952, pp. 81–91.
9. Connolly, *Dates and Documents*, p. 60n.
10. J.C.H. Aveling, 'The Eighteenth Century English Benedictines', in E. Duffy (ed.), *Challoner and His Church*, London (Darton, Longman & Todd) 1981, pp. 165–66.
11. (D. Rees), 'Reduced Circumstances', *The Raven* (Downside School magazine) 63 (1973), p. 24.
12. N. Pevsner, *Shropshire*, London and Harmondsworth (Penguin) 1974, p. 51.
13. Rees, 'Reduced Circumstances', p. 24.
14. Quoted in K. Clark, *The Gothic Revival*, London (John Murray) 1962, p. 97n.
15. P.A. Howell, 'The School Buildings at Downside', *The Raven* 62 (1971), p. 12.
16. H.N. Birt, *Downside: The History of St Gregory's School*, London (K. Paul, Trench, Trübner & Co.) 1902, p. 193.
17. H. van Zeller, *Downside By and Large*, London and New York (Sheed and Ward) 1954, pp. 35–36.
18. W.B. Ullathorne, *From Cabin Boy to Archbishop*, London (Burns & Oates) 1941, p. 36. In the novitiate Ullathorne was edified 'with the true spirit of the missionary life'.
19. D. Rees, 'The Benedictine Revival in the Nineteenth Century', in D.H. Farmer, ed., *Benedict's Disciples*, Leominster, Herefordshire (F. Wright Books) 1980, p. 302.
20. For an evocation of the period see A. Morey, *David Knowles: A Memoir*, London (Longman & Todd) 1979, pp. 1–59.
21. C. Fitzgerald-Lombard, *A Guide to the Church of St Gregory the Great: Downside Abbey Near Bath*, Stratton-on-the-Fosse, Somerset (Downside Abbey) 1981, p. 4.
22. R. O'Donnell, 'Pugin's Designs for Downside Abbey', *Burlington Magazine* 123, no. 937 (April 1981), pp. 231–32.
23. The building history of the present church has been discussed in detail by A. James in *The Story of Downside Abbey Church*, Stratton-on-the-Fosse, Somerset (Downside Abbey) 1961.
24. Pevsner, *North Somerset*, p. 183.
25. P.F. Anson, *Fashions in Church Furnishings 1840–1940*, London (Studio Vista) 1965, p. 255.
26. See Morey, *David Knowles*, *passim*.
27. F. Brittain, *Latin in Church*, London (Mowbray) 1955, pp. 69–70.
28. Anson, *Fashions*, p. 281.
29. James, *Story of Downside*, p. 6.
30. S. Leslie, *Cardinal Gasquet: A Memoir*, London (Burns & Oates) 1953, p. 263.
31. 'Odds and Ends', *Downside Review* 56, October 1938, p. 23.
32. The patronage and construction of new churches outside Downside under Benedictine inspiration could usefully provide the basis of another study.
33. See n. 23.

The School and Monastery Buildings at Downside

Peter Howell

When the exiled monks from Douai arrived at Stratton-on-the-Fosse in 1814, there were two buildings on what is now the site of Downside Abbey.[1] The three-storey Mount Pleasant (now known as the Old House) was built about 1700 in an old-fashioned style, covered in yellow stucco, with mullioned windows on the south front and sash windows on the east, where the entrance porch stood. Behind stood an older farmhouse, also of three storeys, although much lower. It was demolished in 1897 after a fire, apparently along with a gabled building (perhaps a chapel) at the north-east corner of the Old House. The latter suffered in 1921–22 from a crude extension on the east, and from a remodelling in the 1960s, which gave it a new roof and more or less gutted the interior. Its stout staircase survives.[2]

In the year of the move the monks commissioned their first design for new monastery buildings, from John Tasker (c. 1738–1816), the elderly Catholic architect of the chapel at Lulworth Castle, Dorset, and of Spetchley Park, Worcestershire. (In the same year Tasker re-fronted Acton Burnell Hall, Shropshire, where the monks had found refuge in 1795.) The design at Downside was for a large, plain, square block, but it did not find favour with the community. Drawings by Tasker survive for a chapel in classical style, but with a 'Gothick' ceiling, and a Gothick tabernacle on a sarcophagus altar.

In 1819 Sir John Coxe Hippisley of nearby Ston Easton, well known in Catholic circles through his work in Parliament and as an envoy to the Holy See, recommended a young former pupil of Sir John Soane, George Allen Underwood (1793–1829) from Cheltenham.[3] Underwood produced three designs for new buildings, one classical and two Gothic. The most striking (and the only one to survive) involved building a copy of the Old House further west, to be used by the school, linked by a large Perpendicular chapel to the Old House itself, which would be used by the monks.

Hansom's round tower is set off by Scott's completion of the abbey tower. The dominance of the abbey tower is enhanced by the sloping site.

The architect finally chosen was H.E. Goodridge (1797–1864), although his building (see opposite) has been altered. A clumsy passage in the same style around the west end (known as the 'North-west Passage') was added in 1867. The floor running across the 'nave' windows was removed in 1876 when this space became the Petre Library, with doors and furniture designed by the Hon. Revd William Petre (1847–1893) himself (see p. 45), but has since been replaced. The tall pinnacles that crowned the chapel front were removed in about 1910.

In 1882, after the first part of the abbey church was built, the chapel became the school museum, and later a classroom and also a dormitory. Its stone altar, with deep-cut carving, was moved to the undercroft of the church in 1888. It has since been destroyed, but the stone statue of Our Lady can still be seen there (without its 'beautiful, rich canopy'). The chapel reverted to ecclesiastical use in 1933 as the Junior House chapel, when its decoration was much simplified by Dom Hubert van Zeller. The plaster arcading on the sanctuary walls has recently been revealed, but sadly the stained glass in the south windows (of purple and gold interlacing pattern), presented by Count Mazzinghi, was smashed when the chapel was used as a dormitory. It now houses the fine alabaster statue of the Virgin and Child carved for the abbey church by Alfred B. Wall in 1883, and a magnificent crucifix in brass and lapis lazuli signed '*Petrus Paulus Spagna fecit Romae 1845*'. 'Petrus Paulus Spagna' may have been the son of Giuseppe Spagna, bronze founder and goldsmith, who restored the statue of Marcus Aurelius in Rome. The crucifix was given by Sir Alfred Tichborne, an Old Gregorian.

By 1838 the community – no doubt a little ashamed of Goodridge's 'incorrect' Gothic, when compared with the much more learned understanding of Gothic that had been current in that decade – was thinking of further expansion. It is not surprising that the monks contacted the twenty-six-year-old A.W.N. Pugin (1812–1852), who made his first visit in September of that year. He must have thought it one of the greatest opportunities of his life. In his first scheme, of October 1839, he proposed to Gothicize the Old House, and to run a new front northwards from its eastern side for 300 feet (91.5 m). There would be a towered gatehouse in the centre, a tall, grand refectory with hooded fireplace and open roof, a library, twenty cells, a novitiate and offices, all arranged around a spacious cloister.

The interior of the Old Chapel in its glory days. It remained the principal place of worship for monastery and school until 1882, and now serves as a school chapel.

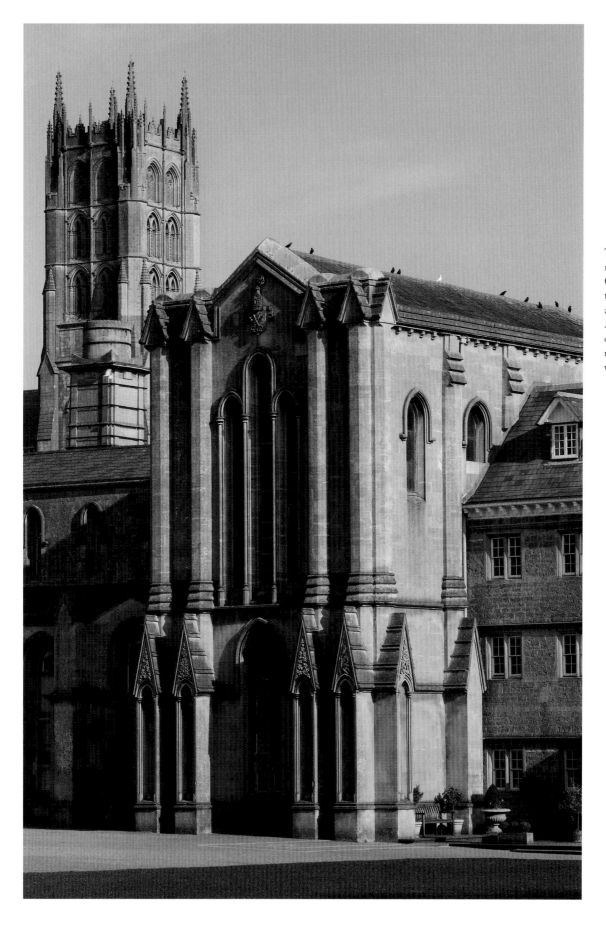

The Old Chapel remains much as designed by Goodridge, but without the pinnacles that once adorned the south front. A scheme in the latter part of the twentieth century to replace them in fibreglass was not pursued.

This comparatively modest scheme was succeeded in December 1841 by a far more grandiose one, also by Pugin, with four courtyards: the monastery cloister with the office (or lay brothers') court to its north, and to the west of the first the school quadrangle, with guest quarters to its north. Along the south side of the cloister ran the vast church, 300 feet (91.5 m) long, Early English in style, with one spire over the crossing and two at the west end. The cloister would have had carrels along the south walk, the chapter house and calefactory to the east, and the refectory to the north.[4]

It was intended to make a start with the kitchen court and the north and east cloister walks, and stone was prepared for the purpose. Nothing was built, however, and the stone was used on the Downside farm. An expected legacy did not materialize until 1844, and Pugin's plans had meanwhile come in for much criticism. The placing of the monastic buildings to the north of the church would have made them dark, and alarm was expressed at the proposal to demolish the existing structures. Pugin's answer was that the latter was not intended at present, although the church would eventually be built on the site of the existing buildings. He wrote to the prior, Dom Peter Wilson, on 4 December 1841:

> I feel assured [that] on further reflection you
> will see the utter impossibility of changing
> the position of the church unless the whole
> of the present buildings were demolished before
> commencing the work[,] which is the very thing
> we have contrived to obviate. I do not think
> with so large a quadrangle you will find any
> inconvenience by being to the northward
> of the church. I could find you hundreds of
> examples of it among the most celebrated
> abbeys and religious houses.[5]

Later critics pointed out that the scheme took no account of the changes in ground level. In the end,

Pugin's only contributions at Downside were some items of church plate, supplied by Hardman of Birmingham, and the design for the monastery seal (1846), which is still used as a bookplate for school prizes.[6]

Meanwhile Charles Hansom (1817–1888), younger brother of the better-known Joseph Aloysius Hansom (1803–1882), had produced designs in 1844. This may have been at the suggestion of one of the monks, Dom Bernard Ullathorne, who was parish priest of St Osburg's, Coventry. Ullathorne had his own church built by Hansom in 1843–45, and took him on trips to Europe. After becoming Vicar Apostolic of the Western District in 1846 (living at Clifton, Bristol), he commissioned Hansom to reconstruct Goodridge's Pro-cathedral there (now replaced by Clifton Cathedral). As a result Hansom set up practice in Clifton that year or the next. Ullathorne (who became the first Bishop of Birmingham in 1850) encouraged his fellow-priests to employ Hansom rather than Pugin, whom he regarded as extravagant and impractical. Nevertheless Prior Wilson wrote to Hansom in 1844 that 'we have not given up hope of having Mr Pugin as our architect'.[7]

In March 1846 Hansom produced a proposal for a new monastery and church at Downside. As at Woodchester Dominican Priory in Gloucestershire, where he replaced Pugin in the same year (again, probably, on Ullathorne's recommendation), he seems to have been shown his predecessor's designs. At Downside he suggested keeping the existing buildings and running a wing north from the Old House, as in Pugin's first scheme, but for only half Pugin's intended length (just 150 feet/45.7 m). This turned west along the southern side of the church – which was only 195 feet (59.4 m) long, and with just a crossing spire – and then ran south to join the block of 1823. The school buildings were on the western side.

In November 1846 financial problems brought to a halt all building projects (until Downside became an abbey in 1899 all such proposals had to be approved

A detail of the Tichborne crucifix showing its bold colouring. It is now in the sanctuary of the Old Chapel.

SMYTHE HOUSE
&
POWELL HOUSE

PARKING

by the ruling body or regimen of the English Benedictine Congregation). Hansom did finally build, in 1853–54, but on a fairly modest scale, and for the boys rather than the monks. The work (using white lias rather than Bath stone) consisted of a western extension to the Goodridge building, with a longer wing running south at a right angle. In the corner was a stair-turret containing the school bell. Ornamental features included the statue of St Gregory in a niche and an oriel window on the south front, the latter doomed eventually to disappear. On the first floor was the large hall known as the 'Palace', where the 'Boy King' held court each Christmas; it is now the Petre Library. The stage (its inscription, 'God save the King', puzzling to Victorian visitors) was designed by Hansom in 1858. The royal throne, which was later used as the abbot's throne and is now in the hall below, was presented by Petre when he became 'King' in 1864. Hansom's work, which is very much in the manner of Pugin, is simple but attractive.

After an abortive revival of the monastery scheme of 1846, Hansom's next project, in 1858, in partnership with his brother Joseph (see p. 38), was proudly engraved for the school prospectus. It proposed a substantial new building attached to the south-east corner of the Old House. Intended for the use of the monks, it was to have a steeply pitched roof and a tall, square tower with an octagonal top stage. Nothing came of it. Charles Hansom's only other executed works were the Ballplace of 1854 (a splendid stone structure for the playing of a long-defunct game that mystifies visitors) and St Benedict's Church, Stratton-on-the-Fosse (1857; see pp. 28–29). His charming design of 1859 for an observatory was not executed (the observatory destroyed by fire in 1867 was simpler).

By 1868 Charles Hansom's firm was called 'Chas. F. Hansom and Son', as he had been joined by his son Edward Joseph Hansom (1842–1900). Educated at Downside in 1855–58, Edward had worked in the

The Hansom school building has spacious halls and public spaces on the ground floor and accommodation on the first floor. Teaching, recreational and dormitory space are integrated in the Downside school buildings as well as in the monastery.

office of Alfred Waterhouse in 1866–67, and claimed to have made all the drawings for Waterhouse's entry for the London Law Courts competition. In 1867 he became a partner in his father's practice. The extensive collection of letters from Edward preserved at Downside shows that Charles was no longer getting enough commissions to launch his son's career. On 14 August 1869 Edward told the cellarer (bursar), Dom Placid de Paiva, that the firm was doing 'little or nothing', although it had completed several large projects since he joined it, including the rebuilding after a fire of St Paul's Anglican Church, Clifton, and the Franciscan Convent at Woodchester, where he said that he had 'carried out' the chapel himself.

The monks had already commissioned Edward to build a steward's house ('almost complete' in 1868), the building east of the later boys' refectory; a new gateway from the village, with elaborate wrought-iron gates (1870–71; the gates now replaced); and a new chimney piece for his father's 'Palace' (1871). He was, however, desperately anxious to be awarded the plum commission for more school buildings, the monastery and the church, and wrote repeatedly to the prior, his former schoolfellow Dom Bernard Murphy, to that effect. Murphy (prior from 1870 to 1878) was described by Abbot Bruno Hicks as 'a quiet, courteous and most religious man … almost an ideal superior'. His proposal for new buildings was regarded by many of the monks as too ambitious, but it was rewarded by a substantial increase in numbers at the school. Hicks considered that 'great credit and gratitude' were due to him.[8]

In 1870 Edward Hansom told Murphy that the firm had too little work to keep one man employed, let alone two, and his father was urging him to 'secure something' for himself. It appears that the prior had suggested that, if Edward's uncle Joseph Aloysius took him into partnership, Murphy would give Edward the Downside commission. Joseph replied that he was concerned about the career of his own son, presumably John Stanislaus, whom he had taken

into partnership in 1869. Edward was puzzled, pointing out that Joseph had recently refused a partnership with Charles and himself, when 'he [Edward] had as good as got the Downside work in his own hands'. Joseph then urged Edward to apply for a job at H.M. Office of Works, at the same salary (£150) as his eldest son Henry had received at the War Office. Edward indignantly described this to the prior as 'positive starvation', pointing out that Waterhouse had paid him £182, and that Henry had become a mere district surveyor. (Edward was, perhaps, forgetting that his father had begun his career as a district surveyor in Coventry.)

Edward supposed that if he were 'out of the way', the community would employ his uncle, but it appears from a letter written in 1884 by Prior Aidan Gasquet that most of them wanted to employ E.W. Pugin (who had built Downside's House of Studies at Belmont in Herefordshire).[9] Edward explained that he understood that the monks might think him too young to do the work on his own, although at his age (twenty-eight) his father had built Woodchester Priory ('his best work'), and Waterhouse the Manchester Assize Courts, which made his name. Edward accused his uncle of ingratitude, since, when Joseph had found himself 'almost penniless' in Edinburgh in 1854, Charles had provided him with a house, money and a partnership in Clifton. When Charles terminated the partnership, in 1859, Joseph was so offended that he 'took away all my father's best clients'.[10] Despite all this, Edward hoped that the community would help him by giving him the commission, and so enable him to purchase a partnership, for which, he said, a man must bring 'work or money'.[11]

In April 1871 Edward had a stroke of luck, when he received 'an unexpected offer of a partnership' from Archibald M. Dunn (1832–1917) of Newcastle, an old pupil of Edward's father ('by far the cleverest he ever had'). Dunn was building a large church for the Dominicans in Newcastle, and had recently inherited

An exterior view of the monastery, showing the stone staircase at the southern end. The wall in the foreground, contemporary with Charles Hansom's work in the school, was used for a handball game found in various forms in both northern France and Somerset, and at Ushaw.

£60,000 from his father, so he needed no money from Edward, although he did want him to bring work to the office. There was still talk of Joseph acting as 'consulting architect' at Downside, a fact that Edward said Dunn would have to accept. Edward assured Murphy that Dunn was highly praised by Fr King, the Dominican Provincial, whom he had asked to send a testimonial to Downside. Already at this time there came the first suggestion of what was to be one of Dunn and Hansom's principal commissions, the south front at Stonyhurst College in Lancashire (which was mostly Edward's work).

Edward asked Murphy not to tell his uncle about the proposed partnership, but told him about it himself during the next month. Joseph rejected the idea of being 'consulting architect', and at this point behaved in a way that shocked Edward. Exactly how remains unclear; the letter that would have explained it, referred to in Edward's letter to Murphy of 24 June 1871, is missing. It seems possible that Joseph – who had written to someone Edward referred to as 'young English', apparently asking him to write to Dunn – was trying to put a spoke in Edward's plan.

By July 1871 Edward had moved to Newcastle. In 1872 Joseph visited him at Tynemouth, and Edward reported that he still wanted Downside 'all for himself'. Edward, however, had by now drawn a plan – 'I am certain my uncle could not make a better'. In April it appears that Dunn and Hansom were finally being given the commission. Edward suggested to Murphy that, if he intended to write to Joseph, Murphy should let Edward know so that he could see Joseph first. This is the last reference to Joseph in the correspondence. It is clear that he considered it unfair that his nephew had been shown favour because he was an Old Gregorian. Ten years later Prior Gasquet reminded Edward that he had been employed 'at your most earnest entreaty in a letter to Fr B. Murphy … You were a Downside man, and he wanted to give you a good turn.'

By August 1872 Edward was preparing final plans, and asked if a bird's-eye view was wanted. He argued strongly against giving the monastery three storeys, which would preclude 'a monastic feeling'. In March 1873 his perspective of the interior of the church and the bird's-eye view were being photo-lithographed. The originals were sent to the Royal Academy of Arts in London, where that year a perspective of the exterior of church and monastery from the north-east was hung; it was also illustrated in *Building News*.[12] It shows the east wing of the monastery, with sacristies next to the church, a projecting chapter house and the monks' refectory, separated from the boys' refectory by a buttery. The library was to be a very large building running east–west, attached to the monastery by a westward continuation of the north walk of the cloister. (The bird's-eye view was not hung or published until 1879; see p. 89.[13]) In April 1873 tenders were sought for the foundations of the monastery and school buildings, and that of Barnsley (who was building St Bernard's Seminary at Olton in the West Midlands for Edward) was accepted. The foundation stones of church, tower and monastery were laid on 1 October 1873 by Archbishop Manning and Bishops Brown and Clifford. By 1875 the west wing was being roofed in and the east wing, including the kitchen offices, had begun. The contractor was Joseph Blackwell of Bath.

The first phase of Dunn and Hansom's work consisted of two storeys of the monastery, including the west cloister, linked to the school by the south cloister one level below, the school refectory with dormitory above, and the passages between the south cloister and Charles Hansom's block of 1853–54. Edward Hansom had suggested putting another cloister above the south one, and a storey of cells above that, to avoid having a third storey on the monastery, but it was considered essential to leave this side empty.

The boys' refectory (1873–76; see p. 48) was parti-cularly splendid. In his book of 1902 Dom Norbert Birt wrote: 'It is impossible by mere verbal description to do justice to the excellence of the proportions of the baronial hall'.[14] The elaborate stone chimney piece has a relief apparently carved by William Farmer showing the attempt by St Benedict's monks to poison him, and mosaics in the spandrels were made by Minton's to a cartoon by George Bernard Maycock of Hardman, Powell & Company.[15] The windows are filled with armorial glass. The pitch-pine panelling was one of the numerous benefactions of Petre, who, as an architectural enthusiast living at Downside from 1874 to 1877, participated in all details of the Dunn and Hansom design, always tending to prefer great elaboration.[16] He also gave the brass gasoliers, which were later moved to the sacristy. The south, or Petre, cloister is a conspicuous example of his taste, with its lavish stone-carving and heraldic glass. Another is the open-air swimming bath (1874–75), which also bears his name; its timber changing loggia (now, sadly, vandalized) is delightfully ornate. The dormitory that survives above the refectory, reached by a spiral staircase with a picturesque pointed roof, was once a remarkable period piece, but has changed its use and lost its fittings (p. 49).

Unfortunately the new school buildings were left with some raw ends, to which unworthy temporary buildings were added. In 1884, to the west of the 'Yard' corridor, a classroom building was reconfigured as the substandard Gasquet hall. At least it was built of stone, unlike the monastery guest wing, the 'White House' (now replaced by Francis Pollen's wing; see p. 210), on the east side of the cloister garth; or the gymnasium, built in 1911 of a material ominously (but – as it turned out – inaccurately) called Eternite (the building was destroyed by fire in 1955).

The monastery, which was first occupied in 1876, has large and impressive rooms on the ground floor – the calefactory, chapter house and what used to be the library – and rows of cells above. Over the porch, which projects on the west, was a chapel. Two additional storeys were added later, in two phases: the northern half before 1892 and the rest in 1899–1900, to a revised design; the southern end was given a square battlemented tower instead of gables. A short 'sanitary wing' added in 1899 at the north-west corner is known as the 'Diu Quidem' from the stone over the entrance commemorating the Benedictine Congregation's new constitutions, which are so-called. The west cloister has bands of darker Ham Hill stone in the vaulting. The carver of all this work was John Roddis of Birmingham; floor tiles were supplied by William Godwin & Son of Lugwardine, Herefordshire, and the roofs were of Penmoyle slate.

The question arises of how Dunn and Hansom divided responsibility. The school tradition is that 'Dunn saw that it was handsome, and Hansom saw that it was done', and there may be an element of truth in that, since Dunn spent a great deal of time travelling abroad, and was a brilliant draughtsman. In 1886 he published *Notes and Sketches of an Architect*, subtitled 'A Collection of Sketches made in England, France, Germany, Italy, Spain, etc., and also in Eastern Countries'. Dunn and Hansom's work is sober and severe, although with some picturesque touches. Their grand interiors, and especially the church transepts and Lady chapel, show an impressive handling of scale.

The rapid rise in the number of boys in the school under the headmastership of Dom Leander Ramsay (from 100 to 200 between 1902 and 1914) made further accommodation essential. Ramsay's choice of architect was inspired. Leonard Stokes (1858–1925) was the son of Scott Nasmyth Stokes, an early member of the Cambridge Camden Society, who became a Catholic in 1845, and in 1871 was appointed senior inspector of schools.[17] Leonard was articled to the Catholic architect S.J. Nicholl, and later worked in the offices of T.E. Collcutt, J.P. St Aubyn, and Bodley and Garner. He built a number of fine churches, such as St Clare's, Sefton Park, Liverpool (1888–90), and did much work for convents, most notably the Anglican All Saints Convent, London Colney,

OVERLEAF
The monastery, school and church are constructed together. As the church and school develop, the visual dominance of the monastery, except on the approach from Chilcompton, is lost. The photograph dates from between 1892 and 1899.

The main school refectory was a social centre for the whole Downside community in the nineteenth century. With its pine panelling, it was richly appointed with a great stone fireplace and heraldic glass. It reflected the halls of Oxbridge colleges and Victorian stately homes rather than medieval monasteries. It is a statement of Downside's 'collegiate' ambitions.

Hertfordshire (1899–1902; now the Catholic All Saints Pastoral Centre), the entrance tower of which is very similar to that at Downside, but more vigorously modelled. Considering his father's profession, it is not surprising that he showed a special gift for educational buildings. North Court at Emmanuel College, Cambridge (1910–14), is the best known, but the finest are at Downside.

Stokes was the first Catholic to be elected President of the Royal Institute of British Architects. His official portrait, by Sir William Orpen, shows him in a dressing gown, which shocked many people but was characteristic of his downright and clear-minded nature. He was notorious for his quick temper. It is not surprising that he was one of the most original architects of his time: in the words of Nicholas Taylor,

the peculiarly tense austerity of the Stokes style is always unmistakable and seems to show the utmost self discipline of a naturally violent personality. The many-mullioned windows are left bare and unchamfered; the bulk of rock-hard stonework is banded and striped with mathematical precision; everything is hard, angular, unsentimental – giving exactly the feeling of timeless tradition which the soft sentimentalists of neo-Tudor at that time so unaccountably (to themselves) missed.[18]

Charles Rennie Mackintosh described him as one of those producing 'living designs for living men'.[19]

In 1907 Stokes was asked to design a school for 350 boys at Downside, and his scheme is shown in a fine perspective drawing (p. 53). There were to be two great quadrangles. In the inner one Charles Hansom's block was to be retained, but heightened; the Old House and Goodridge's building were to go. A large gymnasium stretched westwards behind the main entrance tower, and 'Great Schools' (a hall) occupied the upper floor of the wing between the quadrangles. Intriguingly, the drawing shows the abbey church

The 'New Dormitory' of the Dunn and Hansom school building was situated above the main refectory. Spacious, airy and well-lit, it was refurbished at the beginning of the twenty-first century as a conference centre in honour of St Bede. The original partitions and fittings have disappeared.

tower completed, in a manner not unlike that later employed by Giles Gilbert Scott.

Stokes's association with Ramsay was a happy one, as one can tell from Ramsay's obituary of him in the *Downside Review* of 1926. He tells how Stokes took a 'deep personal interest' in the project, welcomed suggestions and 'struggled' to find the best solution to every problem. Their characters were so similar – Ramsay was not a man to suffer fools gladly – that one can imagine how they must have respected each other. A third forceful character involved was the builder, Jacob Long of Bath, who is said to have told Stokes on looking at the drawings that the buildings would not stand up. Stokes was enraged, but had to give in to Long's superior knowledge of the Mendip subsoil; the foundations were duly redesigned.

A start was made on the scheme in 1910 with an L-shaped block attached to the south end of Charles Hansom's building. It was completed in 1912. Although representing perhaps one-eighth of the complete design, it is by far the most distinguished of the school buildings. Stokes used dressed Combe Down stone contrasted with local rubble. The windows are placed almost flush with the walls, emphasising their size, and the roofs were of silver-grey Riding tiles. On the entrance (or Roberts) tower (overleaf) are statues of Ambrose Barlow and John Roberts – two of St Gregory's martyrs of the Reformation. The *Downside Review* claimed that the building's Jacobean style recalled the period of the foundation of St Gregory's, but it is doubtful whether this was Stokes's intention.[20] Carving was by Abraham Broadbent of London, and plasterwork by George Jackson & Sons.

With its light, tunnel-vaulted corridors 12 feet (3.7 m) wide (see p. 62), its spacious classrooms and the lavish use of African walnut for panelling and stairs, the block set a new standard. The three floors represented recreation, teaching and sleeping. The two great dormitories on the top floor, measuring 60 by 35 feet (18 by 10.6 m) but each containing only twenty-four beds, were lit by narrow windows at the bedsides and long dormers above, and were presided over by statues of the patrons of the new 'houses', Abbot Caverel and Roberts.[21] They were remarkably attractive rooms. Stokes had a passion for detail, and loved to design door fittings, light switches and so on. Evidence of this can be seen in his drawings at Downside, which include elaborate designs for the shower-bath fittings, the towel horses, the blackboards and even the adjustable desks, of which Ramsay was particularly proud.[22]

An article in the *Architectural Review* of 1912 was full of praise: 'The ventilation of the classrooms is quite perfect, and one can imagine under what excellent conditions the boys work.' One ingenious idea eventually went by the board, however: 'In the recreation halls on the ground floor each boy has a good-sized locker, numbered, and this number carries him throughout the whole building – his desk, bed, school-book locker in the first-floor corridor, washing-place and other accommodation being all similarly numbered.' Another was perhaps never sufficiently appreciated:

> In the lavatories [wash-rooms] a wire screen
> divides the room into two parts, and around
> this screen are arranged some lines of hot-water
> piping for the towels. When towels, however,
> are put over round pipes there is a tendency
> for them to drop off. To overcome this defect a
> strip of iron about an inch wide is fixed upright
> on the iron piping, and this simple device
> effectively grips the towels and prevents them
> falling on the floor.[23]

The First World War put a stop to building activity. Afterwards Stokes produced, as a work of love, a new and revised design, which was referred to by Ramsay in his obituary of Stokes (some drawings

The Petre cloister, endowed by Monsignor Lord Petre, is richly encrusted with carvings and has a striking series of gargoyles. Its dramatic west end has an arresting and much-photographed skull, which embodies the Petre motto, *Sans Dieu Rien.*

RIGHT
The Roberts tower as designed by Leonard Stokes, a beautifully drawn concept wonderfully executed. The figure in the foreground resembles a bedesman from an almshouse rather than a monk.

OPPOSITE
Stokes's vision for a renewed Downside consisted of a splendidly balanced and elegant series of buildings and courtyards dominated by an abbey church with a restrained tower.

PAGES 54–55
The school quadrangle, only a fragment of the Stokes plan, has striking fenestration and beautifully finished stonework. The Roberts tower, designed to be the centrepiece of the never-completed Stokes building, dominates the school buildings and gives them a visual centre.

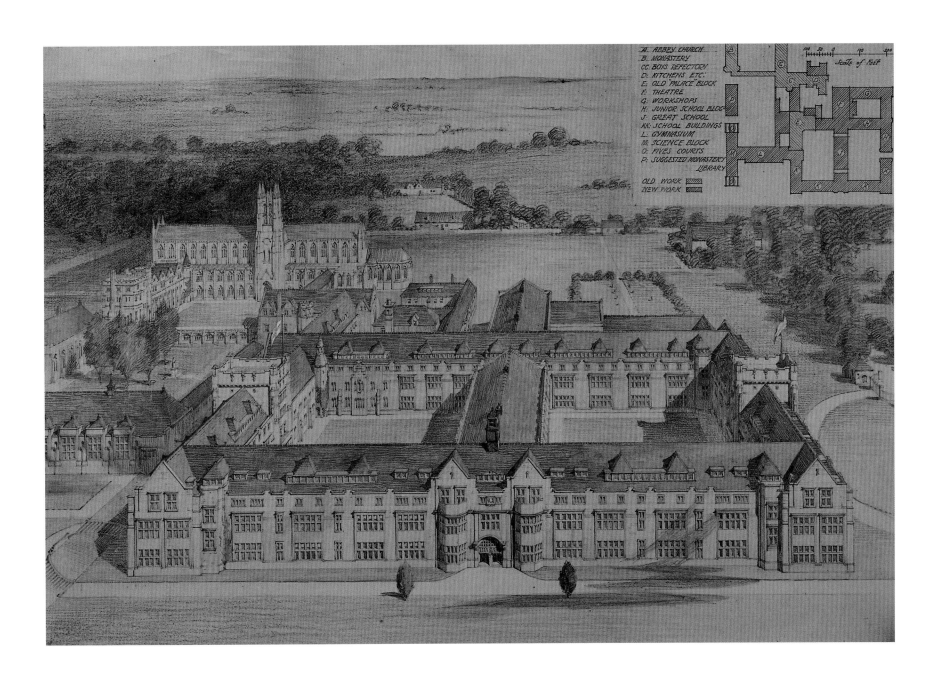

A. ABBEY CHURCH
B. MONASTERY
CC. BOYS REFECTORY
D. KITCHENS ETC.
E. OLD PALACE BLOCK
F. THEATRE
G. WORKSHOPS
H. JUNIOR SCHOOL BLDG
J. GREAT SCHOOL
K. SCHOOL BUILDINGS
L. GYMNASIUM
M. SCIENCE BLOCK
O. FIVES COURTS
P. SUGGESTED MONASTERY LIBRARY

OLD WORK
NEW WORK

Scale of Feet

of 1920 and 1925 survive). Stokes's only other substantial work at Downside (he probably designed the great chimney for the heating system) was the Allan swimming bath of 1926. He had died the year before, after suffering for a number of years from the paralytic illness that had gradually prevented him from working, and so the Allan was no doubt the work of his firm, led by his former pupil George Drysdale. Stokes had also, in 1914, produced a fine design for a new church for the Downside parish of Radstock, but it remained unexecuted.[24]

It is unfortunate that the exigencies of change have led to many alterations to Stokes's buildings, which were not listed until 1989. The great corridors have had to be interrupted by fire doors, and leaded windows have been insensitively replaced. Worst of all, the Caverel dormitory has been subdivided.

In 1924 the Bristol architect George Oatley (1863–1950), who designed the astonishing Wills Memorial Building at Bristol University and was knighted in 1925, produced a design for new monastery buildings.[25] He proposed a refectory and chapter house opening on to the east cloister, and three storeys of rooms above the south cloister. In a report Oatley claimed that his scheme had the approval of Stokes and Ninian Comper.[26] In 1925 Abbot Ramsay proposed two alternative schemes: 'one for a quad-rangle diagonal with the present one and extending to the back of the ball-place, the other for a quadrangle west of the existing buildings, its northern arm running out from the monastery porch'. Not surprisingly, this seemed too ambitious, and Ramsay proposed the building of a wing on the south side of the garth, 'on the lines of the plans prepared by Sir George Oatley in 1924'.[27] This was accepted by the chapter, but came to nothing. In 1928 a larger version of the scheme was suggested by Dom Roger Hudleston and modified by Oatley, who proposed that the south end of the monastery be lengthened, and the front of the south cloister moved forwards. Presumably the community decided that it wanted the view of the church from the south kept open. In 1929 Oatley proposed an extension of the monastery to the south, on the same axis, with a large new block and short wings running west. None of this came to anything.[28]

In 1932 Sir Giles Gilbert Scott (whose nave for the abbey church had been completed in 1925) built the science wing (pp. 60–61), running west from the small stump – now the common room for academic staff – behind Stokes's entrance tower. The wing is in a plainer and squarer style than Stokes's. It is remarkable that, despite being an original and inventive designer, Scott displayed extraordinary tact in adding to buildings by other architects. He showed it again in 1939, when he finished off Stokes's wing at its eastern end. His addition is not symmetrical, and the changes of level inside are awkward (owing to the significant new provision of a large number of private rooms), but it is very successful. It included a dormitory for Barlow House at the top.

The only other pre-war structure that requires mention is the cricket pavilion of 1931, a straight-forward but characterful design by the accomplished amateur architect Dom Ephrem Seddon (who also designed the Stratton-on-the-Fosse war memorial).[29]

A minor alteration of 1946 was the moving south of the facade of part of the corridor past the boys' refectory, to form a refectory for the junior house. No architect was involved.

By the 1950s new buildings were becoming a necessity. In 1953 the Liverpool firm of Weightman & Bullen (later to be architects of the celebrated church built for the Ampleforth parish of Leyland, Lancashire) produced designs for a new refectory on the site of the school's lavatories opposite the Gasquet hall, and for changing rooms west of the hall, but these were not executed.

The fire of 1955 providentially destroyed the temporary gymnasium and 1920s junior house dormitories, which were in any case due to be

OPPOSITE
The Stokes and Hansom buildings represent a contrast in both architectural and educational styles. Stokes's work makes a statement about forward-looking ideals, while Hansom's evokes a lost Gothic ideal.

BELOW
Dom Ephrem Seddon (1883–1966), who was articled to an architect in Liverpool, was a monk of Erdington Abbey from 1908 and came to Downside in 1913. This is one of Dom Hubert van Zeller's 'family portraits': affectionate cartoons of the Downside community dating mainly from the years between the two world wars.

The Gregorian martyrs, John Roberts and Ambrose Barlow, are patrons of two of the school's houses and were canonized in 1970. Both are represented in the stonework of Stokes's building: Barlow in his monastic cowl, and Roberts in the Eucharistic vestments in which he was arrested in 1610. They reflect the chasuble of twentieth-century Downside rather than seventeenth-century London.

replaced. The first new structure, however, was Brett, Boyd and Bosanquet's northward extension of the science wing, a workmanlike Modern building (1957–58). The same firm was responsible for the large new development between the older buildings and the Allan swimming bath. Built in 1958–61, it contained two new houses (including classrooms), a theatre complex and a gymnasium. Although these buildings used a certain amount of stone walling, they were otherwise typical of the light modernism of the period. By 1959 Lionel Brett (Lord Esher) had dissolved his partnership with Kenneth Boyd and Peter Bosanquet, and soon afterwards he went into partnership with Francis Pollen (see pp. 201–215).

The most substantial recent building is the Girls' House, Isabella, which opened in 2006. It was designed by NVB Architects of Frome and reflects the building of 1958–61, but with more use of glass.

An interesting summing-up of the community's attitude towards building was provided by Hudleston in an article in the centenary issue of the *Downside Review* (1914). He argued that there had always been a dislike of 'building for building's sake', that schemes were regularly postponed, and that the community had been determined to get what it, rather than the architect, wanted. (The most remarkable instance of this came later, when Scott had to produce three designs for the nave of the church before the monks were satisfied.) Furthermore, he said, there was a general preference for simplicity; Petre's buildings were an exception, but reflected his taste. When Hudleston's summary was mentioned to the head-master, Dom Aelred Watkin, in the 1960s, he at once agreed, arguing that the monks had always known better than their architects. Although Watkin was deliberately exaggerating, there is an element of truth in his comment.[30] And there is another way in which the monks regularly resisted change: existing buildings were almost never demolished to make way for new ones, unless they had been damaged by fire.

Giles Gilbert Scott's school building stretches west from the Stokes block. With its Cotswold tiled roof and robust stonework, it is more country house than collegiate.

Stokes's elegant school corridor with its barrel-vaulted ceiling, leading to well-lit classrooms, reflects the best in contemporary educational architecture.

1. Much of the information in this chapter comes from the collection of drawings at Downside. The letters referred to are in the Abbot's Archive. Useful articles in the *Downside Review* include three by 'A Gregorian Jubilarian' (Dom Alphonsus Morall): 8 (1889), pp. 168–91, 9 (1890), pp. 125–55, and 10 (1891), pp. 187–98; Dom Roger Hudleston's article 'Buildings' in the centenary issue, 'with Record of a Century' (33, 1914, pp. 142–70); and nos 28 (1909), 29 (1910), 31 (1912), 39 (1921), 40 (1922) and 44 (1926). This chapter also makes use of P. Howell, 'The School Buildings at Downside', *The Raven* 62 (1971), pp. 11–18.

2. I. Jessiman, 'The Old House' (1961), typescript in Downside Abbey Library. He does not mention the gabled building. The parlour (or kitchen) panelling had already gone to the church of the Downside parish of Midsomer Norton, converted from a barn by Giles Gilbert Scott (his first work for Downside) and opened in 1913.

3. Underwood refers to Hippisley in a letter dated 21 September 1819, recently discovered in the Downside Archives.

4. The scheme was published in the *Dublin Review* in February 1842 (in an article reprinted in 1843 in A.W.N. Pugin, *The Present State of Ecclesiastical Architecture in England*, London

(Charles Dolman) 1843, pp. 105–107); see R. O'Donnell, 'Pugin's Designs for Downside Abbey', *Burlington Magazine* 123, no. 937 (April 1981), pp. 231–32, and below, pp. 85–88.

5. M. Belcher, ed., *The Collected Letters of A.W.N. Pugin*, I, Oxford (Oxford University Press) 2001, p. 296.

6. Information from the Hardman Archive supplied by the late Shirley Bury of the Victoria and Albert Museum, London.

7. H.N. Birt, *Downside: The History of St Gregory's School*, London (K. Paul, Trench, Trübner & Co.) 1902, p. 219.

8. B. Hicks, *Hugh Edmund Ford: First Abbot of Downside*, London and Glasgow (Sands & Co.)

1947, p. 21. Murphy was later a great support to Ford in his efforts for monastic reform.

9. Prior Gasquet to Edward Hansom, 28 November 1884. Gasquet was prior 1878–85.

10. Penelope Harris (to whom I am grateful for help with the history of the Hansom family) thinks this accusation is unfair: 'Joseph was an excellent networker with many contacts, and it does seem that Charles felt he had been pushed down a secular route because of Joseph's success' (conversation with the author).

11. Edward said that a Downside monk (Dom Ephrem Guy, who served for a time at St Anne's, Edge Hill, Liverpool) had suggested he should go

into partnership with an 'overworked architect' called Kirby – presumably Edmund Kirby, who set up practice in Liverpool in 1865.

12. *Building News* 24 (30 May 1873), p. 616. A view of the interior of the church was published in 1874 in *The Architect* 11 (17 January 1874), p. 36, and a view of the choir in *Building News* the same year (27, 16 October, p. 413). In 1883 another view of the church was hung at the Royal Academy; see A. Graves, *The Royal Academy: A Complete Dictionary of Contributors and their Work from its Foundation in 1769 to 1904*, London (Bell), vol. 2 (1905), p. 389.

13. *Building News* 36 (13 June 1879), p. 660.

14. Birt, *Downside*, p. 234.

15. Edward Hansom to Murphy, 3 February, 6 May and 27 May 1876; Minton's estimate, 1 May 1876.

16. S. Foster, 'A Pillar of Downside: Lord Petre', *Symposium of the History Commission of the English Benedictine Congregation*, Stratton-on-the-Fosse, Somerset (Downside Abbey) 1988–89, pp. 4–19. Petre succeeded to the title in 1884.

17. On Stokes, see P. Howell in *Oxford Dictionary of National Biography* and J. Ward, *The Leonard Stokes Directory: Architect in a Dressing Gown* (J. Ward) 2009. Stokes's nephew Richard Rapier Stokes (son of his brother Philip) was the first head of the school under the new system of prefects at Downside, and later became Lord Privy Seal.

18. *Architectural Review* 140 (1966), p. 200.

19. P. Robertson, ed., *Charles Rennie Mackintosh: The Architectural Papers*, Cambridge, Mass. (MIT Press) 1990, p. 207.

20. 'Opening of the New School Buildings', *Downside Review* 31 (1912), p. 210.

21. The 'house' system was introduced at the school with the completion of the Stokes buildings. In common with much of the arrangement of the building, it reflected the educational ideas of the headmaster, Dom Leander Ramsay.

22. H. van Zeller, *Downside By and Large*, London and New York (Sheed and Ward) 1954, pp. 75–77.

23. *Architectural Review* 32 (1912), pp. 228f.

24. A perspective drawing is in the collection at Downside. Other unexecuted works for which drawings survive include a gymnasium and science block to run wet from the new entrance tower (1910); urinals south of the Yard (1911); a new 'temporary dormitory' to run south from the dormitory over the boys' refectory (1914); a new monastery library, with two extra storeys over the Petre cloister (1914); a wing running east from the boys' refectory (1916, later revised); and an infirmary (1919).

25. On Oatley, see S. Whittington, 'The Pride of Bristol, and an Enduring Monument to the Genius of Sir George Herbert Oatley', in K. Ferry, ed., *Powerhouses of Provincial Architecture 1837–1914*, London (The Victorian Society) 2009, pp. 61–73. Dr Whittington is preparing a book on Oatley.

26. *Ibid.*

27. Bristol University Archives, Special Collections, Oatley MSS, Report (1924).

28. Material relating to these schemes is in the collection at Downside, and there are also drawings and correspondence in the Oatley archive in the Special Collections of Bristol University Library. In 1929 Oatley reported that the new abbot had scrapped the plans and that new ones were being prepared. There are nine drawings dated July 1931, along with a plan dated May 1924. (Information from Dr Whittington; see n. 25.)

29. Seddon was said to have worked for an architect in Liverpool. Whether he was related to the architect John Pollard Seddon is unknown.

30. An exception would have been made by Abbot Hicks, who blamed 'amateur architects at Downside' for putting pressure on Thomas Garner to substitute a triple east window in the church for the single window he preferred (see pp. 136–40).

Henry Edmund Goodridge and the First Buildings at Downside

Amy Frost

When the community of St Gregory the Great purchased the estate at Downside in 1814 it comprised 21 acres (8.5 ha) of land with an assortment of estate buildings and a late seventeenth-century mansion house. A proposal to build new accommodation for both the monastic community and the school was immediately made. Over the course of six years, during a period of uncertainty when the community explored other locations in England and abroad in which to settle permanently, three different architects submitted proposals for a new building. The final decision to remain at Downside resulted in the acceptance of the third scheme for the new school and chapel, to the design of Bath architect Henry Edmund Goodridge (1797–1864).[1]

In 1820 Goodridge was just embarking on his professional career, and Downside was not only one of his first major commissions but also his first work in the developing area of Catholic building in England. For twenty years from the time of his employment at Downside, Goodridge would be involved in three of the most significant pieces of new Catholic architecture (see p. 82), and of those three buildings only his plans for Downside would be fully realized.

The early phase of expansion at Downside has been largely neglected, mainly for lack of evidence in the form of either original drawings by Goodridge or records of his work on the school and chapel.[2] Letters in the Downside Archives reveal much about the design process for the new building and the progress of its construction. The use of this material in the context of Goodridge's developing architectural style makes sense of both Goodridge's design and the aspirations of the Downside community.

When Goodridge embarked on his designs for Downside he was following unexecuted schemes submitted by John Tasker (see p. 35).[3] Tasker was an established architect who worked primarily for Catholic clients, and it is likely that plans for the neoclassical building he proposed for Downside were

H.E. Goodridge's rural idyll: Downside in 1823 as Prior Park's country cousin. The ornamental monk is more Beckford than Benedictine.

drawn up before or immediately after the community moved from Acton Burnell Hall in Shropshire, the home of the Smythe family, whose alterations included Tasker's re-facing of the house with a Greek Revival facade and Ionic portico.[4] It was most likely while working on the alterations to Smythe's house that Tasker was consulted about a new building for Downside, and it is possible that he drafted the scheme without having even viewed the site. Plans for constructing a new building went no further in 1814, but by January 1819 fund-raising was well under way and a new architect was being sought.[5]

In 1819 a series of variant designs was produced by George Allen Underwood (1793–1829).[6] A letter written by Underwood on 27 June 1819 suggests that his Downside designs were based on sketches rather than a site visit, and it is possible that those sketches were Tasker's designs of 1814.[7] Alternatively, he could have been sent recommendations drawn up by the monks themselves. Underwood wrote that he had endeavoured to follow the sketches, 'making only those alterations as I consider advisable'.[8] In perhaps the most significant point of his proposal, he conveyed the importance of joining the old house to the new, rather than creating separate buildings: 'I recommend the new building be faced to corner bond with the old both for economy and appearance[,] and the height of the floor must of course be kept about the same.'[9] Underwood's designs for Downside included one that proposed to replicate the original mansion, linking the two 'matching' buildings with a Gothic chapel.

While Underwood's proposals were being considered and donations continued to be received, the question of whether the community was to remain at Downside, let alone construct new buildings there, was still under discussion.[10] In November 1819 Dr Bede Brewer of Downside reported to Dom Michael Lorymer in London that Prior Bernard Barber had been in the capital on business concerning the 'prospective purchase of property in place of

Downside', and plans for the construction of a new building at Downside were again put on hold.[11]

It was not only the plan for relocation that caused postponement. Discussions over proposed parliamentary legislation regarding Catholic emancipation were also at the forefront of the community's concerns, and in February 1820 Brewer suggested that no further advances on new building should be made until emancipation was in place.[12] Embarking on a new building, which would be the most ambitious monastic architectural project since the Reformation, at the height of a debate on emancipation would have made that building a symbol of the status of Catholicism in England.[13]

While hopes of embarking on a building to celebrate the emergence of a more open Catholicism would have been in his mind, Brewer was perhaps reminded of the immediate need for greater accommodation for the school and monastery. The pressure of the growing community soon saw the search for new property resume. During the early months of 1820 Burton Hall, a three-storey red-brick manor house dating from *c.* 1750, near Christchurch in Hampshire (now Dorset), was surveyed as a potential new property, and in February Dom Augustine Harrison and Dom Bede Polding were sent to Christchurch to view it.[14]

Harrison and Polding dispatched a series of rough sketches of Burton to Downside, detailing the east entrance elevation, the west elevation and plans of all three floors marked up to show suggestions of how the rooms could be used by the community.[15] By March 1820 the move to Burton was looking more viable, and permission was sought to purchase the house at an estimated £2600.[16] The owners of the estate soon increased the pressure for a decision, resulting in Barber inviting Dom Peter Augustine Baines of the Bath Catholic Mission to advise on Burton's suitability.[17] It was an invitation of which Barber 'soon [had] reason to repent'.[18]

Elevation.

Baines had taken an interest in the potential of Downside since its purchase by the monks, and in 1814 he had written from Ampleforth to the prior of Downside concerning his ideas for a new college; he had even drawn out his own plans and enclosed them for the prior to view.[19] Having designed some of the alterations at Ampleforth, Baines was acknowledged as having a degree of expertise in architecture, and that resulted in his being consulted on architectural matters at Downside.[20]

In 1809 the Catholic Mission in Bath had purchased the old Theatre Royal building in Old Orchard Street and set about converting it into a new chapel.[21] When Baines moved to Bath from Ampleforth in 1817 he soon recognized the need for larger accommodation for the Mission, and over the next two years he made a series of additions and alterations to the chapel.[22] A letter from Barber to Lorymer reveals a great deal about both the final decision to remain at Downside, and the tense and uncomfortable relationship between the community and the ambitious Baines.[23]

Baines strongly recommended leaving Downside, but Barber felt that rather than wanting what was best for the community, Baines wished to remove it from close proximity to his own Mission in Bath. Barber reported: 'In my first conversation with Baines on the subject I discovered my error and have reason to suspect that he wishes at all events to get us out of their vicinity – for the last six years he has never ceased to speak of this house [Downside] in the most contemptible manner, calling it a dog-hole.'[24]

Baines's professed dislike of the Downside property did not, however, stop him from recom - mending to Barber that it would suit an order of nuns to whom he would recommend the building if St Gregory's would quit it. Barber responded with great restraint: 'I made no verbal reply, but I believe he read my inward thoughts in the outward expression of my countenance'.[25] Two weeks later the move to Burton was abandoned and plans to build at Downside revived.[26]

While the counsel of Baines concerning the move from Downside had been disregarded, his advice concerning the design of the new building was still sought. It was he who recommended the architect finally chosen for the new building, Goodridge.[27]

Born in 1797, Goodridge was the son of Bath builder James Goodridge, who had been involved since 1794 in the development of the Bathwick Estate for the Pulteney family. From 1808 until 1835 James had acted as agent for William Henry Vane, Third Earl of Darlington, and in partnership with the architect John Pinch the Elder he was responsible for the development of several properties in Bath, most significantly New Sydney Place (1808), the terrace that introduced early nineteenth-century neoclassicism to the Bath townhouse, and where the young Henry Goodridge grew up.[28] It was from this partnership between his father and Pinch on the Bathwick Estate that Goodridge received much of his early education in architecture, before being articled to Bath architect John Lowder.[29]

In 1819 Goodridge left Lowder's office and set himself up in practice at 7 Henrietta Street.[30] His career spanned more than forty years, until he retired in 1857, and he was best known for the design of Lansdown Tower in Bath, built for the writer and collector William Beckford in 1826–27. Goodridge was also responsible for a series of Picturesque villas on Bathwick Hill, several parish churches in Somerset and Wiltshire, and a new library and alterations to Hamilton Palace in Lanarkshire, Scotland.[31]

Goodridge's stylistic development took him from strict Greek Revival at Argyle Chapel, Bath (1821; now the United Reformed Church), through the immensely influential Greco-Italianate design of Lansdown Tower, to the Picturesque villa style, and finally early Victorian Eclecticism at the Percy Chapel, Bath (1854; now the Elim Pentecostal Church). What makes his work at Downside so significant is both its position at the very start of his career, and the way in which it established him as an architect of new Catholic buildings.

It was probably while he was working in the office of John Lowder that Goodridge first encountered the future Bishop Baines. When making the extensive alterations to the Catholic chapel in Old Orchard Street, Baines recorded in his journal that the architect employed to undertake the work was Lowder.[32] The alterations included the design of a small new chapel to the rear, and the distinctive tall, round-headed windows of this enlargement – recognizable from subsequent buildings by Goodridge – suggest that he may have been responsible for some of the architectural work at the chapel.[33]

In June 1820 Barber wrote from Downside that although the design had yet to be finalized, 'a very agreeable architect has been over above once to examine the premises and is employed in getting acquainted with every building'.[34] Although he did not name the architect, a week later Barber confirmed that it was Goodridge who had been employed, and offered an insight into the architect's desire to secure the commission:

> In speaking of the architect above I omitted to mention that Mr Goodridge, whom I have employed as architect, as soon as he has finished his plans will have them estimated and give any security we please that he will execute them for some £3000 (as he is just commencing in business and wishes to establish his reputation)[;] he will give us one half of his own profits and not charge for travelling expense. He is a young man of considerable talent and activity and very ambitious of making a figure in his profession.[35]

Following so soon after the uncomfortable situation that had arisen from the knowledge that Baines desired the removal of the Downside monks, it was with great reluctance that Barber consulted Baines on his opinion of the new building scheme.[36] It is possible that at this time Underwood's plans were still being considered as the basis of any new design, and that those were the ones Baines was shown. Even though Barber was prepared to reject any advice Baines gave, there was one suggestion Baines made that Barber acknowledged had merit: the proposal to build in the form of a quadrangle.[37] The scale Baines proposed, however, was too elaborate and too expensive. Barber noted that Goodridge would produce two schemes – one according to Baines's ideas and one to Barber's own – showing the community that he had 'a great idea of Baines' taste and judgement in architecture but [saw] that he discards economy'.[38]

The quadrangle form Baines suggested represented the collegiate building style, which would have appealed greatly both to him and to the community at Downside. Collegiate architecture would give the school and new chapel an identity that would liken it to well-known seats of learning, in particular the colleges of Oxford and Cambridge (institutions that Catholic students were prevented from attending). Collegiate architecture also had echoes of pre-Reformation monastic buildings, with courtyards and cloisters that would have had attractive associations when employed in new designs. For Baines to suggest such a form reveals his own ambitions to create a Catholic school and seminary that could become a Catholic university, a desire he would partly achieve in 1829, when as the newly appointed Vicar Apostolic of the Western District he purchased the Prior Park estate in Bath and established Prior Park College.[39]

That the collegiate style appealed to Barber is unsurprising. He would have recognized, as had Baines, the importance of using the building type to define the new school, especially when considering

LEFT
In this view of the school of around 1890, the Old Chapel, with its pinnacles, appears a pastiche compared to its vigorous neighbour, by Charles Hansom.

OVERLEAF
The Old House and Old Chapel alongside the Hansom building, as seen across the fields. The ensemble was clearly visible from the Fosse Way before the visual centre of the site moved up the slope to the new abbey church. The buildings are now overwhelmed by their oversized neighbours.

Bishop Augustine Baines (1787–1843), Vicar Apostolic of the Western District. Despite being a Benedictine, he was Downside's bête noire in its early years. He was reburied in the abbey church, where his tomb was designed by Frederick Walters. It is a fully Gothic tomb for a man whose preferences, revealed at Prior Park, were profoundly Classical.

that the new building would not only strengthen the community against more criticism from Baines, but also establish Downside as the first major new Catholic architectural work in England since the Reformation. (It was to be much more picturesque and imaginative than the colleges at Old Hall Green in Hertfordshire and Ushaw in County Durham, which replaced the closed English College at Douai.[40]) Plans of 1820 to build an entire quadrangle of buildings may have been too ambitious considering the funds available, but what emerged in Goodridge's design can be viewed as one range of a potential quadrangle, to which further ranges could, and eventually would, be added.

On 21 June 1820 Goodridge wrote to Barber to inform him that his plans were finished but that estimates had yet to be completed, and he noted that Baines had seen and approved of the plans.[41] That suggests that Goodridge did not actually produce two variant schemes, but concentrated on the less elaborate one; perhaps he realized that to produce one following Baines's suggestion would be a waste of time, since he knew it would be rejected.

On 27 July Barber reported: 'Everybody that I have shown the plans to are quite delighted with them'.[42] Although there had been delays in obtaining formal permission to begin building, the weather had been too good not to take advantage of, and he had presumed to begin the work on Goodridge's designs. The foundations were complete by 5 August 1820, and Barber congratulated himself on the quality of bricks produced at Mogg Hill on the Downside estate as the result of an agreement made in 1819.[43]

To the west of the Old House Goodridge designed a chapel and school range, producing a south facade that had the appearance of a nave and aisle.[44] The style is Early English Gothic, defined by the triple arrangement of tall, slender lancet windows on the chapel front and the west elevation, and in the octagonal corner tower that terminates the school range. The nave-and-aisle arrangement created a

horizontal building that also had a central vertical focus, and, despite the incongruity between Goodridge's new building and the old mansion, together they created what can be viewed as a range that could form one side of a quadrangle in the collegiate style. The inspiration for 'nave' and 'aisle' can be traced to Goodridge's former master, Lowder.

It can be assumed that Goodridge had access to Underwood's previous schemes for Downside, in particular the suggestion of bonding the Old House to the new structure, and this defined the floor levels of the new building, as Goodridge incorporated the old building into his design. What immediately stands out is that, rather than replicate the Old House as Underwood did, to create a symmetrical and balanced facade, Goodridge made no concession to designing the new to fit harmoniously with the old. By placing the new building to the west of the existing house he created a chapel that was orientated south–north. He made it even more unusual by placing the chapel on the first floor, with a library and refectory below. It was most likely that he was merely looking for a way to make provision for the library and refectory – the two largest rooms required for the school and monastery – while still producing a development of reasonable size and therefore reasonable cost.

A plan of the Goodridge building as it was in 1838 clearly illustrates the two storeys of the range and what the rooms were to be used for.[45] What it also shows is the service wing extending north from the west end of the building. There is very little reference to this element in the archives by either the community or Goodridge, and only a small part can be seen in the engraving of the building in 1844. Considering its use, it is likely to have been added to after 1823, and was not of sufficient aesthetic importance to have an impact on the crucial element of the scheme, the south facade.

By joining the Old House to the new building and placing the chapel on the first floor, Goodridge allowed access between the buildings on two levels while giving the school's five windows the appearance of a tall aisle elevation, despite the fact that they spanned two storeys. Lorymer noted in 1822, when the building was nearing completion, that the windows must have been inconvenient because those on the first floor started at floor level: 'The architect seems to have consulted chiefly the exterior appearance rather than the interior convenience.'[46]

The statement has much validity. Goodridge had effectively designed the equivalent of a Commissioners' church, the form that defined new Church of England buildings during the early nineteenth century. Following the Church Building Act of 1818, which aimed to increase the number of local churches and therefore the ability to preach to as large a congregation as possible, the Commissioners' church style evolved as a large box, normally quite plain, but some - times with a fairly elaborate entrance front. Since strict limits had been set on the cost of new churches, the entrance front of a Commissioners' church became the only opportunity for architects to display their talents, and where much of the expense was spent.

Goodridge's Downside chapel and school can be viewed as a design in the Commissioners' tradition, but one where the aisle elevation sits alongside the entrance front, rather than behind it. Similar to the Commissioners' need to fill a new church with as many pews as possible, one of Goodridge's priorities at Downside would have been to arrange the school accommodation to provide as many rooms as possible within the budget. The result was that, as with the Commissioners' churches, and just as Lorymer accused him of doing, Goodridge placed the emphasis of his design (and, no doubt, most of the expense) on one facade.

In 1820 Goodridge was in his second year of practice, and had little experience of church building. The Commissioners' church was the dominant form at that time and the most accessible from which he could draw influence. It is also understandable that he

followed this new Church of England style, since there were few new Catholic churches from which he could take inspiration.

Goodridge himself might not have chosen Gothic for Downside, since after establishing himself in practice he rapidly showed a greater interest and ability in the neoclassical. The Church Building Act Commission had advocated the use of the former, however, since it was deemed ecclesiastically and financially more appropriate than the neoclassical, and perhaps Goodridge also knew that Gothic would find favour with the community at Downside because it was not the preferred style of Baines, who favoured monumental Roman architecture. More significantly, Goodridge's choice – coming twenty-one years before the publication of A.W.N. Pugin's *The True Principles of Pointed or Christian Architecture* (1841), which advocated Gothic for ecclesiastical buildings – won him favour with the community because of the style's religious and nationalistic associations.

The recognition of Goodridge's use of the 'national style' in 1820 was strongly reinforced in the *Downside Review* of 1890, when his design was highly praised as being 'far far ahead of its days when it was built', and possessing a great ability to inspire those who inhabited it: 'What could appeal more strongly to the mind and heart, to the feeling and imagination, of young men who, although not yet free from the possible infliction of penal laws, were just rising from beneath the crushing weight of two hundred years of frightful persecution, than a building which would always remind them of their glorious past?'[47]

Goodridge's knowledge of Gothic architecture by 1820 had come from a combination of sources, mainly through academic study rather than practical experience. While a student he had made an extensive survey of the Perpendicular Gothic of Bath Abbey, and shortly after submitting designs for Downside he also produced plans for the proposed enlargement of St Thomas à Becket Church in Widcombe, Bath, a structure dating from 1490.[48] The publication in 1817 of Thomas Rickman's *An Attempt to Discriminate the Styles of Architecture*, the first study fully to classify the periods of Gothic architecture, had been immensely influential to the Commissioners' churches, and it was there that Goodridge probably gained much of his academic knowledge of the Early English style he employed at Downside.[49] He reinforced this theory by studying Salisbury Cathedral, the influence of which is clearly seen in the chapel and the west facade of the school at Downside.[50]

In the year Rickman's work was published Goodridge undertook an exercise in the Gothic when he made a watercolour of a Gothic mansion in a landscape setting.[51] A fanciful and highly Picturesque view, it illustrates the extent of his understanding of Gothic when he approached the Downside commission, and explains why his school and chapel at Downside have a Picturesque Gothic quality rather than displaying an extensive knowledge of Gothic forms. Goodridge's understanding of the style increased after his work at Downside, with his restoration of Malmesbury Abbey (1822).

Following Downside Goodridge designed a series of Anglican parish churches in Somerset and Wiltshire, in the Commissioners' tradition. Elements of the Downside chapel, in particular the four pinnacles with stylized finials seen in the early views but removed in 1910, are also seen in his designs for Christ Church, Rode Hill (1824; now closed) and the Free Church in Frome (1836–39). Not being Goodridge's preferred style, although it offered him a sense of 'artistic feeling', Gothic was employed by him mainly for religious buildings, with the exception of Devizes Castle (1838) and his entry for the Houses of Parliament competition in 1836.[52]

Progress on the new buildings at Downside was not as rapid as the community had hoped. By April 1821 the school had reached two storeys and the chapel was 'fast raising above the floor'.[53] By May 1821 construction was moving 'more briskly than it has at anytime [*sic*] since last summer', and by July the school was almost complete. The chapel, despite having a further 20 feet (6 m) to go, had already attracted interest from outside the community: 'Persons come from far and wide to view the building[;] it is the admiration of the county.'[54]

However, by February 1822 the chapel was still incomplete and there were concerns that it would not be ready to open before the end of July.[55] The community had to wait yet another year before it was finally finished and officially opened on 10 July 1823, after three years of construction and at a cost more than twice the original estimate. For the next fifteen years, very little building work was executed at Downside, and although subsequent works have greatly affected the interior of Goodridge's building, his design has externally been little altered, with the striking exception of the removal of the four slender pinnacles from the roof of the chapel.

Goodridge's influence at Downside did, however, continue after the completion of the work on the new building. In 1835 Polding, who had been involved in the discussions over Burton Hall in 1820, went to Australia to take up the post of Vicar Apostolic of New South Wales. Polding appears to have taken with him a portfolio of designs by Goodridge, which he used to build churches following the Early English style of Downside, including St John the Evangelist in Richmond, Tasmania.[56]

What is perhaps most significant about Goodridge is that – unlike most of the architects who would design additions to the monastery and school – he was not Catholic. He was actually a long-term and active member of the Nonconformist congregation of the Revd William Jay based at the Argyle Chapel in Bath, a building Goodridge had enlarged in 1821.[57] It seems that unlike Pugin, who from 1839 followed him with designs for Downside, Goodridge did not wish to infuse his Gothic with deep ecclesiological meaning.

The crosses of Goodridge's staircase to the Old Chapel, on the first floor, suggest an ecclesiastical use.

The vault of Goodridge's Old Chapel was repainted in 2000 by Philip Bouchard, an Old Gregorian artist, to reflect the night sky.

Instead it was a conscious combination of historic forms and those of his own invention, visibly associated with a traditional English religious structure while also recognizably of the nineteenth century.

Goodridge's career as a non-Catholic architect of Catholic churches continued after the completion of Downside when in 1836 he was commissioned by Baines to design St Michael and St George in Lyme Regis, Dorset. There he again used the Early English style of Downside.[58] In his designs for other buildings for Baines, however, he would employ a very different style.

The lack of building at Downside between 1823 and 1838 has been blamed on the extensive and high-profile works Baines undertook during the 1830s at Prior Park in Bath, for which Goodridge was largely responsible.[59] Baines commissioned Goodridge in 1829 to convert the mansion house of 1734 by John Wood the Elder into a new seminary and school.[60] Following his lack of control over the community at Downside, Baines's ambition at Prior Park, which he had purchased in the year of emancipation, was to create a Catholic college and (in future) university that would visually proclaim the strong presence of the Catholic Church and be the centre of the Western District.[61]

Meanwhile Goodridge was also commissioned to design the Church of the Twelve Apostles in Clifton for the Catholic Mission in Bristol (1831–36).[62] Taking inspiration from Baines's preference for large-scale Roman architecture, and his own exploration of the Greek Revival, Goodridge designed a Greco-Roman temple surrounded by giant Corinthian columns and with a lantern over the crossing. The church's position on the edge of a quarry caused structural difficulties, however, and by 1836 building work had been suspended, leaving only the crypt and up to two-thirds of the exterior walls.[63] The tragedy of Goodridge's Bristol church, which – following Charles Hansom's additions from 1846 – became the Clifton Pro-cathedral, was that it would have been the first new large-scale Catholic church since the Reformation. As a ruin it held little influence over the further development of either Catholic church design or ecclesiastical architecture in general.

The unrealized ambition of the Twelve Apostles in Bristol was repeated at Prior Park when in 1836 Goodridge designed for Baines a large domed Corinthian chapel intended to sit behind the original mansion house and stand tall, overlooking the whole valley and city of Bath. Its sheer scale highlights the nature of Goodridge's and Baines's ambitions. The impact it would have had when seen from the city was no doubt at the forefront of both architect and client's minds. Barber had noted Baines's disregard of economy during the discussion of his suggestions for Downside, and with the chapel scheme at Prior Park it again appeared that financial implications were secondary to the grandeur of such a building.

Had the chapel been constructed, the glory of the Catholic Church would have been proclaimed to all in a manner that was a far cry from the hidden worship of the early eighteenth century and the back-street chapels of the early nineteenth. As a sign of power and dominance and a new show of strength for the Church, it would have been the most significant Catholic church in post-emancipation England. With the Church of the Twelve Apostles (had that ever been completed), it would have made Goodridge one of the most influential architects of new Catholic churches in England. But these two Greco-Roman churches were forever to remain visions, existing only in Goodridge's paintings.[64] Downside was less monumental and less expensive, but no less significant. It would be the only one of Goodridge's grand designs for the re-presentation of Catholic architecture in England ever to be fully realized.

Goodridge's chapel at Downside is approached by a stone staircase with a metal balustrade with appropriate cruciform motifs. The choir stalls and tribunes have been removed, but it remains devotional and well lit. Its scale is modest but spacious: 62 feet

(19 m) long, 23 feet (7 m) wide and about 35 feet (10.5 m) high. It served as the monastic church from 1823 until the opening of the first part of Dunn and Hansom's new building in 1882, and is now the school chapel.

Goodridge's contribution to the buildings at Downside seems minor in comparison with the scale of the additions and church-building that followed. Yet the importance of the first school and chapel should not be dismissed. On completion in 1823, Downside was the most significant new monastic building to have been constructed in England since the Reformation. In its landscape setting it created a Picturesque scene of quiet contemplation, and it imbued the community with a sense of permanence and stability that would endure and continue to grow through the buildings that followed.

1. The main source for biographical details of Goodridge's life is A.S. Goodridge, *Brief Memoir of the Late Henry Edmund Goodridge*, RIBA Sessional Papers, 1864–65, extra pagination 3–5. For a study of Goodridge and his career, see A. Frost, 'From Classicist to Eclectic: The Stylistic Development of Henry Edmund Goodridge (1797–1864)', unpublished PhD thesis, University of Bath, 2009.

2. For the earliest assessment of Goodridge's work at Downside, see 'Round About Downside, XI', *Downside Review* 9 (1890), pp. 125–55. Goodridge's original detail drawings for Downside are referred to in the *Downside Review* 33 (1914), pp. 46–49 and 146–50, as part of an uncatalogued collection including drawings by Tasker, Pugin, C.F. Hansom, Dunn and E.J. Hansom, currently unlocated. See also B. Little, *Catholic Churches Since 1623*, London (Robert Hale) 1966, and R. O'Donnell, 'Roman Catholic Church Architecture in Great Britain and Ireland 1829–1878', unpublished PhD thesis, Cambridge University, 1983.

3. For Tasker see H. Colvin, *A Biographical Dictionary of British Architects, 1600–1840*, New Haven, Conn. (Yale University Press) 1978, p. 1015.

4. For Tasker's alterations at Acton Burnell see a drawing dated 1813 in the Shropshire Record Office, 1514/2/1222.

5. Letter from Lady Throckmorton to Sir John Coxe Hippisley, 26 February 1819, Downside Archives, E.143.

6. A former pupil of Sir John Soane, Underwood was responsible for the rebuilding of the Bath Lower Assembly Rooms, which had been partially destroyed by fire. He retained the earlier Doric portico by William Wilkins and adapted the building that soon became the home of the Literary and Scientific Institution in Bath, of which Goodridge became a member in 1828. For Underwood see Colvin, *Biographical Dictionary*, pp. 1064–65.

7. Underwood to Sir John Coxe Hippisley. Downside Archives, E.167.

8. *Ibid.*

9. *Ibid.*

10. Copies of the list of subscribers to the building fund are in the Downside Archives, E.206.

11. 29 November 1819, Downside Archives, E.197.

12. Letter to Lorymer, 19 February 1820, Downside Archives, E.218. It was perhaps the hope of the resolution proposed in Parliament by the Earl of Donoughmore in May 1819 over the Roman Catholic Claims – which, although rejected, had increased moves towards emancipation – that led Brewer to consider change imminent.

13. Although emancipation was not achieved until 1829, the year Downside was officially opened in 1823 was a significant one in the progress towards emancipation, as it marked the start of Daniel O'Connell's campaign for the repeal of the 1800 Act of Union.

14. Brewer to Lorymer, 28 February 1820, Downside Archives, E.222. For Burton Hall see N. Pevsner and D. Lloyd, *Hampshire*, London and Harmondsworth (Penguin) 1967, p. 158.

15. The sketches are in the Downside Archives, E.223.

16. Edward Bowles (who was acting on behalf of Downside in the Burton matter) to Bede Polding, 2 March 1820, Downside Archives, E.224.

17. Letter from William Baldwin to Edward Bowles urging Downside to 'make up minds' over the purchase of the house, Downside Archives, E.228.

18. Barber to Lorymer, 5 April 1820, Downside Archives, E.321.

19. Baines to Barber, 10 September 1814, Clifton Diocesan Archives.

20. For Baines and Ampleforth see P. Gilbert, *This Restless Prelate: Bishop Peter Baines*, Leominster, Herefordshire (Gracewing) 2006.

21. The Old Orchard Street chapel is now the Bath Masonic Temple. For the history of Roman Catholicism in Bath see J.A. Williams, *Bath and Rome: The Living Link. Catholicism in Bath from 1559 to the Present Day*, Bath, Somerset (St John's) 1963 and J.A. Williams, ed., *Post-Reformation Catholicism in Bath* (2 vols) (Catholic Record Society) 1975.

22. The alterations to the Old Orchard Street chapel are detailed in Baines's journal, which is held in the archive of St John's Church, Bath, and has been reproduced in Williams, *Post-Reformation Catholicism*, pp. 200–58.

23. Barber to Lorymer, 5 April 1820, Downside Archives E.321.

24. *Ibid.*

25. *Ibid.*

26. Brewer to Lorymer, 26 April 1820, Downside Archives, E.235.

27. In a letter to Lorymer dated 23 April 1820 Brewer refers to Baines's

advising on the new building plans. Downside Archives, E.234.

28. J. Goodridge and Pinch signed the New Sydney Place lease, which is in the Bath Record Office, 0044/1/6. Another signed lease indicating that Goodridge occupied the first house in the terrace is in the collection of Lord Barnard at Raby Castle, Co. Durham.

29. The son of a Bath banking family, Lowder has been referred to as 'a wealthy amateur', who in 1817 became surveyor to the city of Bath. His best-known buildings were the Bath and District National School (1816), an interesting circular building with wedge-shaped classrooms, and Holy Trinity Church, St James Street (1819–22). Both have now been demolished. See Colvin, *Biographical Dictionary*, p. 661, and W. Ison, *The Georgian Buildings of Bath*, Reading, Berkshire (Spire Books) 2003, p. 101.

30. Bath Directory of 1819: '7 Henrietta Street, Mr H.E. Goodridge, Architect', Bath Record Office.

31. For a discussion of Goodridge's career and architectural developments, see A. Frost, 'From Classicist to Eclectic', and N. Jackson, *Nineteenth Century Bath Architects and Architecture*, Bath, Somerset (Ashgrove) 1991.

32. For references to Lowder in Baines's journal see Williams, *Post-Reformation Catholicism*: 27 December 1817 (p. 221), 21 April 1818 (p. 229) and 5 July 1818 (p. 236).

33. The windows are forms that were not widely used until the villa style of the 1830s, but which

Goodridge would go on to use extensively at Lansdown Tower in 1826–27, and would continue to use throughout his career.

34. Letter to Lorymer, 7 June 1820, Downside Archives, E.250.

35. Letter to Lorymer, 14 June 1820, Downside Archives, E.252.

36. *Ibid.*

37. Barber wrote: 'The idea of a quadrangle certainly pleased me and does still[,] but not on the scale which Baines proposes[;] it could not be completed for £10,000 as the architect assured him.' *Ibid.*

38. *Ibid.*

39. By 1834 Baines was openly campaigning for Prior Park to be a Catholic university. In his diary (now in the Clifton Diocesan Archives) Dr Brindle (Baines's assistant) recorded a letter of 4 October 1834 from Baines to the Bishop of Liège about Baines's plan for a Catholic university. For Baines and Catholic education see Gilbert, *This Restless Prelate*.

40. For Catholic architecture in England since the Reformation see Little, *Catholic Churches*.

41. Goodridge to Barber, 21 June 1820, Downside Archives, E.253.

42. Barber to Lorymer, 27 July 1820, Downside Archives, E.263.

43. For the agreement concerning the bricks see Downside Archives, E.130. The Prior commented that even though many of the community had regarded the bricks as 'fit for nothing', they were found to be excellent, and he claimed that 'the workmen only complain that they are too good'. Barber to Lorymer, 5 August 1820,

Downside Archives, E.265.

44. This description was noted in *Downside Review* 9 (1890), pp. 125–55, and more recently by N. Pevsner in *North Somerset and Bristol*, London and Harmondsworth (Penguin) 1973, p. 182.

45. Reproduced in *Downside Review* 9 (1890), facing p. 136.

46. 25 September 1822, Downside Archives, E.435.

47. *Downside Review* 9 (1890), p. 128.

48. Goodridge's plan and elevation for the enlargement, as well as details of the project, are in Incorporated Church Building Society records at Lambeth Palace, London, ICBS 261.

49. On Rickman and the influence of his publication see N. Pevsner, *Some Architectural Writers of the Nineteenth Century*, Oxford (Clarendon) 1972, chapter 5.

50. It is noted in *Downside Review* 9 (1890; p. 130) that Goodridge's study of Salisbury Cathedral was his inspiration for Downside. This information was probably provided by his son, Alfred Samuel Goodridge, whom the article's author notes as the source of the details of Goodridge's life.

51. The watercolour is signed by Goodridge and dated 1817. Victoria Art Gallery, Bath, BATVG:P:1909.172.

52. Goodridge's entry for the Houses of Parliament competition in 1836 has not been found, but a written description details a Baronial Hall for the House of Lords and an octagonal House of Commons. See Frost, 'From Classicist to Eclectic', chapter 7. Goodridge's attitude to

Gothic as having some 'artistic feeling' was recorded by his son A.S. Goodridge in *Brief Memoir*.

53. Barber to Brewer, 4 April 1821, Downside Archives, E.330.

54. Barber to Lorymer, 24 May 1821 and 30 July 1821, Downside Archives, E.332 and E.348.

55. Barber to Fr J. Jenkins, 25 February 1822, Downside Archives, E.399.

56. The church was altered extensively in 1859 following Pugin's model, and little of the design attributed to Goodridge survives. See B. Andrews, 'St John the Evangelist's Church, Richmond, Tasmania', puginfoundation.org/index.php?item=file&target=richmondessay. Other churches built by Polding and attributed to Goodridge's designs are St Mary and All Angels, Geelong, Victoria, and St Barnard's, Hartley, New South Wales. See E.J. Kerr, 'Designing a Colonial Church: Church Building in New South Wales, 1788–1888', unpublished PhD thesis, University of York, 1977, vol. 1, pp. 151–63.

57. Goodridge contributed a letter concerning Beckford and Jay to *The Autobiography of William Jay* (1854, pp. 25–29), and his involvement with the congregation can be found in M. Ede, *The Chapel in Argyle Street Bath 1789–1989*, Bath, Somerset (Central United Reformed Church) 1989. In 1854 Goodridge (with his son A.S. Goodridge) also designed for the congregation the Percy Chapel in Charlotte Street, Bath.

58. The Lyme Regis church appears to have been designed by Goodridge without his having viewed the site, and his original tower, which – with its far taller pinnacled roof – formed the focus of the building, has since been replaced by a less dominant design.

59. *Downside Review* 33 (1914), pp. 145–46.

60. For the alterations Goodridge made and his work with Baines at Prior Park, see A. Frost, 'A Bishop's Palace in Bath: Baines, Goodridge and Prior Park', *Bath History*, XII, 2011, pp. 124–37; B. Little, *Prior Park, its History and Description*, Bath, Somerset (Prior Park College) 1975; and Little, *Catholic Churches*, pp. 71–73.

61. For Baines see Gilbert, *This Restless Prelate*.

62. Very few records of the Church of the Twelve Apostles survive. Information regarding its conception and execution was recorded by a priest based at the Pro-cathedral from 1846 until 1928, Mgr Canon Arthur Russell, who sent his recollections of the Bristol Catholic Mission to Bishop Burton (Bishop of Clifton) in 1917. His manuscript is preserved in the Clifton Diocesan Archives. It is in this manuscript, and the interpretation of it by John Cashman, that most of the information on Goodridge's building can be found. J. Cashman, 'The Clifton Mission 1830–1901', unpublished study, 1990, Clifton Diocesan Archives. See also Frost, 'From Classicist to Eclectic'; A. Gomme, M. Jenner and B. Little, *Bristol: An Architectural History*, London (Lund Humphries) 1979, p. 243; and Little, *Catholic Churches*, pp. 75, 102–104.

63. In 1846 Bernard Ullathorne commissioned Charles Hansom to enlarge what remained of Goodridge's building. In 1847 the three-quarters-built Corinthian columns for the portico were removed, and the stone was used in 1850 for the construction of the priest's house. Hansom's design was Romanesque and Lombardic in style and created a curiously planned building that lacks aesthetic coherence. Goodridge's main structure remains but was roofed out, leaving the flanking columns at less than their full height and missing their capitals. Windows were cut into the blank walls, disturbing the temple-like nature of Goodridge's north and south elevations.

64. The view of Prior Park with the proposed new chapel was exhibited at the Royal Academy of Arts in 1835, and that of the Church of the Twelve Apostles in 1836.

The Abbey Church as First Imagined and as First Built: From Pugin to Dunn and Hansom

Roderick O'Donnell

Augustus Welby Northmore Pugin (1812–1852), a convert in 1835, burst on to the Catholic stage in 1838 at the consecration of Oscott College chapel in the Midlands.[1] He probably introduced himself at Downside by calling for one night's stay on 30 September 1838.[2] Although not the first Catholic architect to have been consulted by the community, he was certainly the most famous.[3]

Pugin drew two schemes to rebuild Downside, the first in 1839 and the second in late 1841, which he sent off as 'working drawings' on 17 January 1842. Of these last, a set numbered 1–5 survives.[4] The schemes 'preserved' for the moment the existing buildings, and proposed further building to the north; in the second proposal the existing monastery was eventually to be replaced by a correctly orientated church, thus reversing the usual layout of a monastery to the south of a church. Pugin was adamant on this point, as his correspondence with Prior Wilson shows (see p. 38). So while the plan of the portion of the monastery to be commenced was drawn out in full, that of the church was only partially so, and sketched in as a bird's-eye vignette.

Pugin's proposal for the church was ambitious. His precise medievalism must have come as a shock to the monastic community, which, its late Georgian sensibilities bewildered, was unready to understand or undertake his proposals. The scheme consisted of a towered and spired west front, a spired crossing and an elaborate east end, with the cloister to the north and monastery ranges to the west. Its lancet style (but with wheel windows in the major gables) suggests the sort of primitivism Pugin chose for St Barnabas, Nottingham (1841–44). The proportions are low and spreading, and the window stages of the towers and broach spires cap rather than heighten the aspect. The bird's-eye view (overleaf), which was published in the *Dublin Review* of February 1842 and reissued in *The Present State of Ecclesiastical Architecture in England* (1843), is more hard-edged and more English: the

The north transept by Dunn and Hansom, as built 1879–81.

RIGHT
A.W.N. Pugin, 'On the Present State of Ecclesiastical Architecture in England. Article the Second', in *Dublin Review*, February 1842, plate XIII, 'Benedictine Priory of St. Gregory's, Downside, near Bath'. Bird's-eye view from the north-east, with the church on the site of the existing buildings. Pugin envisaged a monastic complex replete with all the ancillary buildings needed for a full-scale religious house. Downside was never to achieve a grand plan, but Pugin's ambitious scale and quality of detail set a high benchmark, which was attained by successive architects.

OPPOSITE
Dunn and Hansom, bird's-eye view from the south-west. Although labelled 1873, this shows the scheme as intended by 1879.

east window is no longer a roundel but now a tripartite arrangement in plate tracery; buttresses have appeared; the window stages of the tower and the spires have been heightened; the church is no longer squat but aspiring.[5]

Pugin did not publish the plan in the *Dublin Review*, but gave the length of the cloister walk as 150 feet (45.7 m), which would make the church more than 300 feet (90 m) in length. It would have been entered from the west into a narthex, then through a western arch into a ten-bay nave with aisles, with two doors leading from the north aisle to the cloister. There would have been north and south transepts with two pairs of east-facing chapels; the five-bay choir was also aisled with three east-end chapels, but the easterly projection was not to be the high altar. This was enclosed in a four-bay sanctuary, screened between the piers, one of which was directly behind the altar and on the main axis; processional routes led round the sanctuary. This innovative liturgical architecture combined with the many side chapels achieved the endless vistas Pugin desired. The position of the monastic choir – west of the crossing, occupying the last three bays of the nave and forming a church within a church – balanced that of the four-bay sanctuary to the east. To the south of the sanctuary was a hall divided by columns (presumably the sacristy), and to the north a double-aisled chapter house. No window openings are shown in Pugin's designs, but he described his intentions for them as 'in the lancet style'.[6]

Pugin's plans for Downside Abbey Church were really worked out in his scheme for St Barnabas, which occupied him during the winter of 1841–42, and on which he wrote enthusiastically to his patron Lord Shrewsbury.[7] In the *Dublin Review* that revealed Pugin's designs for Downside, he also published three etchings of the Nottingham church, all highly finished, showing the plan, elevation and sanctuary. The last, which he described as 'the chancel', is surrounded by

aisles and eastern chapels.[8] The effect he aimed for at Downside was realized at St Barnabas: the view of the east end of the sanctuary with a central column behind the high altar and the screen vistas through to chapels beyond is an almost exact parallel. The Downside plan shows the choir defined by returned stalls only, with no rood screen or *pulpitum*. At the time of the publication of the *Dublin Review* Pugin revealed a monastic *jube*-screen for the nave of Mount St Bernard Abbey, and a rood and other screens for St Barnabas. Similar examples of Pugin's architectural and liturgical ambitions running away with him would no doubt have appeared in the next working of the Downside scheme.

Pugin was paid a fee of £165 in 1844, and the scheme was still in debate as late as 1846, when lack of funds killed it. His drawings were shown to Charles Hansom, who came up with a derivative lancet-style scheme that same year. Hansom's church was based partly on Pugin's scheme of 1841–42 and even more on a study of the published drawings of St Barnabas. They show a proper *jube*-screen, and the church plan is also given. Like Pugin's, Hansom's church is also sketched into the corner of a plan of the proposed rebuilding of the monastery, but the church is for the first time given a north-easterly position. Unlike Pugin, Hansom did build at Downside, but not a church; that was left to his son Edward.

Edward Joseph Hansom (1842–1900), an Old Gregorian, had a certain entrée, as his letters to his school contemporary (by then prior) Bernard Murphy suggest. Anxious to start an independent career, Edward was articled to his father's practice in Bristol in 1859, but – despite the major commission of St John's Church, Bath (1861–63) from the Benedictines – Charles felt he had not enough work to share. There was also a family rivalry with Edward's uncle and cousin, Joseph Aloysius Hansom and John Stanislaus Hansom.

As he searched for a partner, Edward was approached by Archibald M. Dunn (1832–1917), a member of the Catholic dynasty instrumental in the building and financing of Pugin's Newcastle Cathedral (1844). Dunn wanted Hansom to bring work with him, of which the Downside commission was the most important. Hansom initially joined Dunn in Newcastle while the Downside monastery and refectory were built (1873–76), but by the time the construction of the church was begun (1879) he seems to have run a London office. It appears to have been a genuinely equal partnership: Hansom deferred to Dunn's noted drawing skills, for example, but did not otherwise always agree with him. Letters between Hansom (and sometimes Dunn) and Murphy from 1870 to 1878 give a fascinating insight into the state of a late Victorian Catholic architectural practice, which – with Downside and the rebuilding of Stonyhurst College in Lancashire (1877–89) and of Pugin's Ushaw chapel, Co. Durham (1884) – was rising to prominence very quickly. The Cambridge Church of Our Lady and the English Martyrs (1884–90) would later become familiar to the Downside monks at Benet House, the Downside residence in Cambridge.[9]

To secure the Downside commission, Dunn and Hansom also needed to overcome more established firms, such as that of J.A. Hansom and John Stanislaus, who had built the major Jesuit church in Manchester (1869–71) and Arundel Cathedral (1869–73). The Pugin family was also to be contended with, since E.W. Pugin was virtually architect by appointment to the English Benedictines. Both Murphy and Aidan Gasquet had had the formative experience of their spiritual and liturgical lives as young monks at Belmont, Downside's House of Studies. By 1869 E.W. Pugin's church there had reached a level of architectural and liturgical elaboration unknown in their home priory.[10] There is a tradition that certain members of the community (including Gasquet) wanted to commission Pugin, and certainly the later revisions to the Dunn and Hansom scheme under Gasquet's influence sug-

gested that he liked the great height and elaboration of detail associated with that architect's work.

There was a very full correspondence between Dunn and Hansom and priors Murphy and Gasquet from 1868 to 1885, but only the architects' letters survive.[11] The relating set of architectural drawings is frustratingly incomplete; as is so often the case, there are better records of what was not built than of what was. However, the difference between the 'north country' church designed in 1873 (pp. 92–93) and what could be characterized as 'Gasquet's church', which Dunn and Hansom were prevailed upon to redesign (1879–80) and build (1880–82), stands out. Indeed the similarities are so few that the 'north country' church should be added to the list of unexecuted church schemes, along with those by Pugin and Charles Hansom. The argument can be seen in letters from Hansom and Dunn to Gasquet (who was prior 1878–85). Gasquet is first mentioned in correspondence in 1872, when as 'Brother Aidan' he was to be asked about the levels of the site; as a junior member of the community he was therefore well aware of the 'north country' church scheme.[12] The first letter to him as prior is dated 11 October 1878, and he was thereafter the scheme's most formidable critic, and, it would seem, an unbiddable one. Whereas Hansom's letters suggest that he enjoyed clerical company, and he was quite used to travelling with priests (joining Mgr Edward Consitt of Durham on a journey to Normandy in 1879 and Fr Pirbright S.J. on a tour for sources for the Boys' Chapel at Stonyhurst), an invitation to Gasquet was declined.[13]

The earliest set of drawings of the church that can be identified is that described in a letter to Murphy dated 18 March 1872. Hansom writes: 'The plan I showed you when last at Downside really works out the arrangements of Monastery Church & College conveniently in everyway [sic], and I am certain my uncle could not make a better. I will draw it out in better

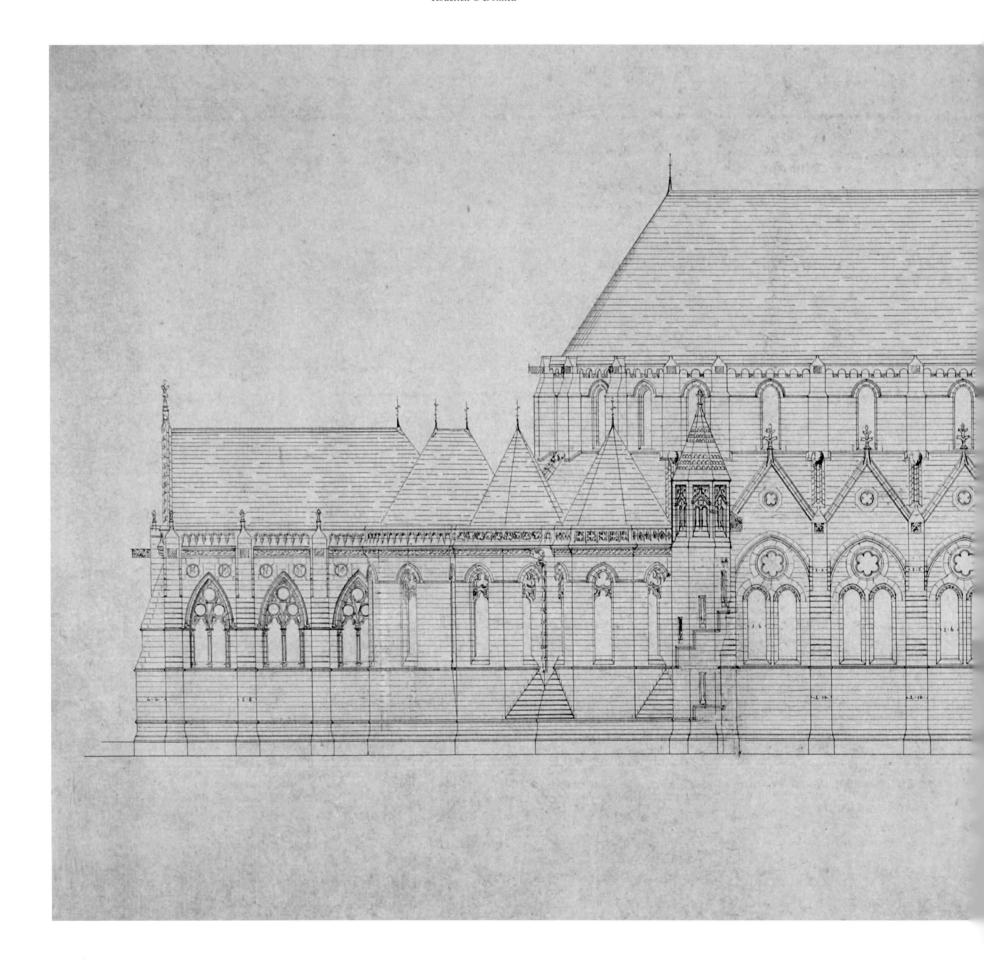

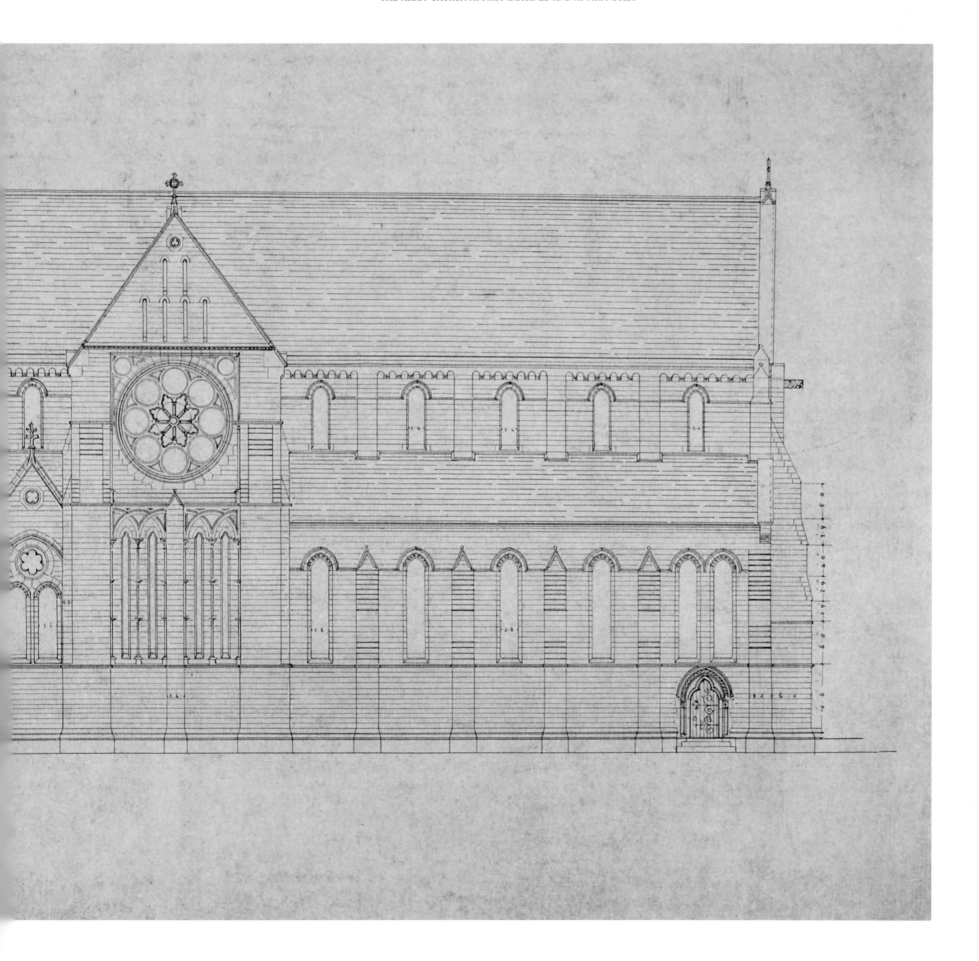

form & send it to you this week.' In an addendum signed 'EJH March 1872' he gives the church's dimensions as 'nave 68 by 30/choir 37 by 30 and sanctuary 37 by 30, but the whole being of uniform height' (perhaps it was not yet fixed). A letter of 3 August 1872 says that a new set of drawings have been done to a larger scale, and that 'birds eyes' are needed, which on 9 August Hansom says will be sent off the next day. These were probably for the Benedictine regimen to see (and indeed 'the bird's eye view … and also the working drawings' were seen by the President General, as Hansom reports to Murphy on 18 March 1873). He writes to Murphy on 22 January 1873 that 'we have nearly all your working drawings ready', including 'a tracing of the interior of the north transept … as a chantry to Dr Morris', and mentions the central column supporting the groining of the vault (see pp. 95–97). The scheme was actually so far advanced that Hansom was able to claim that 'all the drawings are completed to get tenders'. The scheme drawings were also ready to be sent for exhibition at the Royal Academy.[14] These were later reworked as a bird's-eye view (p. 89) to include the south cloister for a prospectus in 1879, but that drawing otherwise appears to reflect the scheme of 1873 (there is, for example, no transept or crossing on the plan). It, too, was offered to the Royal Academy, but with an interesting rider: 'It is doubtful if it will be accepted, on account of the pictures of St Benedict and Our Lady' (in mandorlas hovering over the scene).[15] It was also published in *Building News* in 1879 and in the *Downside Review*.[16]

The church was to be built in stone with tiled roofs, lancet windows and entrances on the north and west. The five-bay nave and aisles were connected by a west–east cloister to the two-storey monastery, from which the church was set back to give a garth to the great west front with its three lancets above an elaborate door. Transepts and a south tower are indicated. The nave was to be vaulted in stone; the lean-to aisles – little more than passages – wooden-

boarded between half arches or struts in stone, with flying buttresses sailing over them and the cloister on the south side. The north side was also drawn out in elevation to show the nave, transepts and choir, the latter flanked by lateral and radial side-chapels, with the hint of a chapel further east.

The architects' proposal was not dissimilar to their own St Dominic's, Newcastle, another austerely detailed and apsed church. A justifiably proud Hansom described its opening, on 10 September 1873, and was able to quote Cardinal Manning's statement that it was a church 'after my own heart'.[17] Manning, who as Archbishop of Westminster was against ambitious building schemes, laid the foundation stone of the Downside monastery church on 1 October 1873, perhaps conveying his approbation in the act. The foundations of the church were not begun until 1879, however, by which time the character and style of Dunn and Hansom's 'north country' scheme were under attack.

When he wrote to Gasquet on 18 March 1879, referring to the foundations having been begun, Hansom was already having to defend the design: 'I think we must educate your taste up to our north country "Early English" as to the shape of the windows, etc; if you once saw the Tynemouth work, you would never care for the more pointed south country work again.' Hansom recommended that Gasquet study Edmund Sharpe's *Architectural Parallels: Or, the Progress of Ecclesiastical Architecture in England, Through the Twelfth and Thirteenth Centuries* (1848), although he might have done well to present it to the client rather than suggest he buy it.[18] It left out Tynemouth, which Sharpe had published as five plates but with no letterpress as *Illustrations of the Priory Church of St Mary, at Tynemouth, an Example of the Transitional Period of English Architecture* (n.d.; *c.* 1850). Hansom's letter also says that 'the drawings were left in the Parlour … I hope you can find them', a curious way to present a scheme to a quizzical client. In his next letter, on 28 March 1879, when the working-drawing stage had already been reached, the 'north country' style was still being defended for its 'vigour', and Dunn's comments on Hansom's drawing were quoted: "'Your composition of the transept is very good but we can only regret that they determined to remove so interesting a feature as the interlocking arches'" (as appear in the drawing on pp. 92–93, but are omitted from that on p. 96). The final defence of the 'north country' design was in Hansom's plea to Gasquet on 26 July for the Tynemouth model and 'the rounder form of arch … a distinct difference in character between the two shapes of arch about as much as between male and female beauty … We had from the beginning conceived … an essentially monastic church … a certain amount of severity of moulding & boldness of lines [as] much bolder & finer in treatment than south country work, and more suitable for a Priory or abbey church.' As well as Tynemouth, its sources were given as Fountains and Rievaulx, both abbeys characterized by their Cistercian austerity and early Gothic or 'Transitional' forms, particularly rounded arches. But Hansom had to conclude weakly: 'The arches shall be pointed more, again.'

Other proposed changes were more radical. As originally intended, the nave and sanctuary arcade had run uninterrupted (as shown on the foundation plans of December 1879; see p. 102), but it was now to be interrupted. Writing to Gasquet on 11 May 1879, Hansom protested against such tinkering, specifically at the crossing: 'The proposed treatment of transepts with the four main arches comes only to the old thing one sees in every cathedral, and … we do not want to look like a cathedral in miniature – we cannot be a cathedral as to size or rival the abbeys of the past.' Dunn's letter to Gasquet of 3 July once again criticizes 'raising the transept arches to the groining' unless it was to support a tower or lantern, just as the practice would do later at Our Lady and the English Martyrs and St Michael's, Newcastle (1891) – but not

at Downside. The great height of the crossing arches makes for one of the weakest aspects of 'Gasquet's church'. Hansom also had to introduce a gallery in the bays, already determined at 14 feet (4.3 m) by the foundations, when he says a width of 18 feet (5.5 m) was needed. What he was now being asked to do, against his own better judgement, was to 'modify to make the whole less severe – point the arches like Westminster & put clustered columns and altogether get rid of any foreign feeling in the detail'.[19] Despite work having started, his letter to Gasquet of 28 May refers to a drawing showing the springing of the groins and details for the tower, and a 'longitudinal section' that showed these alterations, but once again pleads for the integrity of the original design. Hansom and Dunn went church-touring in Normandy in June, and both were subsequently to visit Downside with 'a good deal to say, bearing upon your Church question'.[20]

An element of the scheme close to the architects' hearts was the position of a free-standing column to support the cord of the vault in the north transept, originally intended as the Dr Morris chantry.[21] It was to be 35–40 feet (10.7–12.2 m) high, and the height and proportions of the building had been further debated in a letter to Gasquet of 28 June 1873, in which Hansom cites Dunn as supporting the proposed increase in height: "'*Immense height* … a distinguishing feature between English & foreign styles. I propose to take our own best examples as a pattern, they were *about* twice their width up to the groin – 10 feet [3 m] added would give us this.'" The column was still being defended in Dunn's letter to Gasquet of 3 July 1879 – 'to show it in one of the transepts … the altar for the time being standing against it' – and it appears on the foundation plan shown on p. 102, but in writing to Gasquet on 26 July, Hansom had to concede its omission: 'The central column in the transept, no one seems to appreciate. [It was] once at Fountains, and very beautiful it was.' (Presumably he

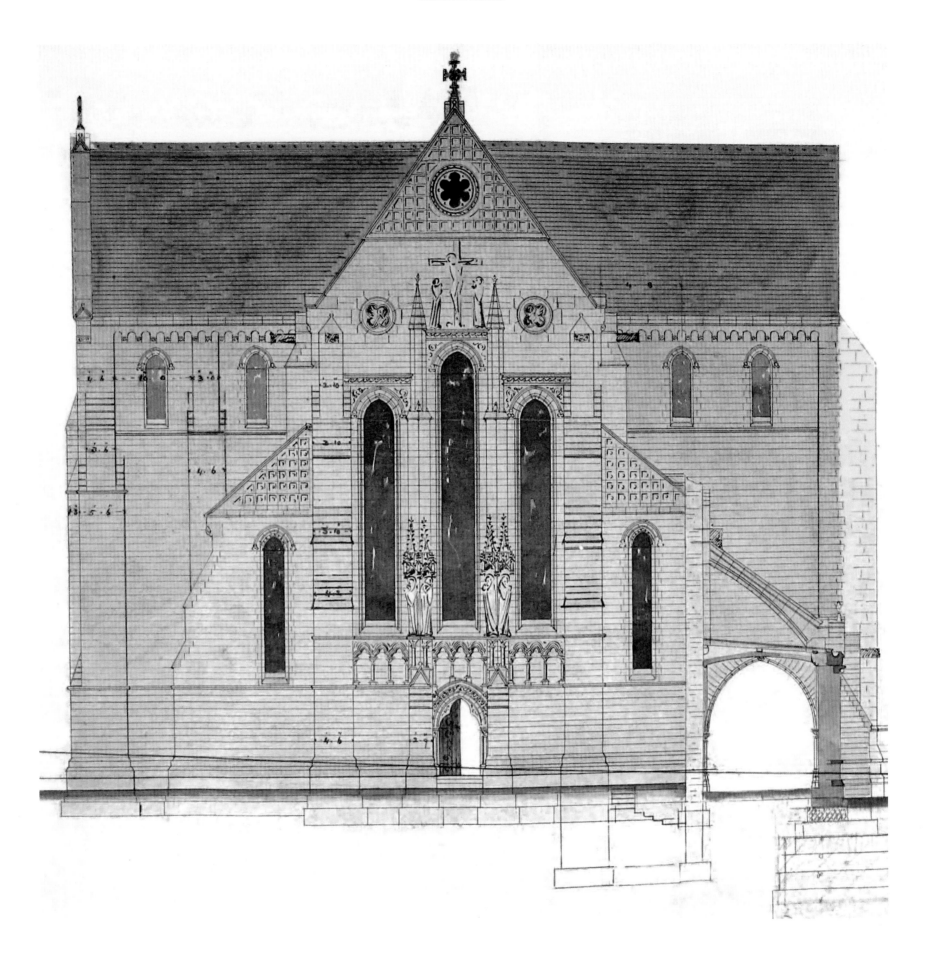

referred to the full-height piers, built to support vaults but later re-roofed in timber, in the chapel of the Nine Altars at Fountains Abbey.)

The 'north country' church was designed in 1873, and the two undated drawings of the nave were probably drawn out in relation to work on the beginning of the monastery. They are the best detailed drawings in the archive, in pen and wash. One is of the nave and transepts in west-end elevation, the long lancets and lancet clerestory windows being the identifying window form of this scheme (opposite). The paired drawing is the section through the five-bay nave and aisles, which were to be vaulted, and to the south, the connection with the monastery (which lay to the west) is shown by a vaulted cloister with chapels above and over-sailing flying buttresses; a south tower is sketched in for consideration (p. 101). The interior of the two-storey nave is austere, with a dado of blind Geometric arches and a five-light arrangement in the west-end elevation.

It seems clear, though, that with the advent of Prior Gasquet, the decision was made to begin not with the nave but with the transepts. Still part of the 'north country' church, a related but incomplete drawing without the coloured washes (pp. 92–93) shows the north elevation: a four-bay nave with lean-to aisles and a four-bay choir with cross-gabled chapels with two-light plate-tracery windows. The lower storey of the transept has interlaced blind arches below a large plate-tracery rose window (with lancets) lighting the clerestory. Hansom quotes Dunn's praise of this transept elevation and its 'interlocking arches' in a letter to Gasquet of 28 March 1879. Gasquet's interest was in how the transept would relate not to nave or monastery but, eccentrically, to choir and east end. The corresponding foundation plan (p. 102) shows the transepts and east end still at four bays, and elements of the 'north country' scheme – such as the lack of a crossing, the single pier in the north transept and the

piers with only one shaft – survive. Significantly, the plan has been marked in blue wash in another hand so as to differentiate the central bays to be undertaken first. All the above drawings, then, must pre-date Hansom's defensive letter to Gasquet on 11 May 1879 (see p. 95). Thereafter such primitivism was first set aside and then overlaid by elaboration (see, for example, p. 105). This process can be seen in the transept drawing on p. 99, where the lower lights are now plate-tracery, two-light windows (with further alterations in pencil), and the clerestory lancets are replaced by two-light Early Decorated windows with tracery heads. Dunn's reported comment on the removal of the 'interlocking arches' in the letter of 28 March 1879 (see p. 95) must give an *antequam* date for the drawing.

For Gasquet, to proceed with the transepts scheme, details of the south tower were also needed. The undated drawing 'St Gregory's Monastery Downside elevation of the spire etc', at a scale of 8 feet to 1 inch (about 1 m to 1 cm) shows this; such a drawing was promised at 1/8 scale in a letter to Gasquet of 27 October 1879, and the working drawings on 3 November, the architects even detailing the spire to a height of 260 feet (79 m). Said to be based on 'Caen' (St-Pierre), in north-eastern France, it must have been the fruit of a trip to Normandy made by the architects in June 1879. The letter continues: 'We are busy redrawing the elevation[,] & sections of the church will necessarily be a work of some time.' The letter makes a distinction between this work and 'the original design' as drawn out in Dunn's sketchbook, which had been lent to Gasquet and is now asked to be returned.[22] Dunn's letter of November 1879, on more alterations to the tower design, marks the further demise of Tynemouth as a model: 'We … have toned down the severe beauty of the Tynemouth work by introducing some of the more elaborate work (as in the Ladye chapel) of the next later period', here citing Tintern Abbey.[23] (Other

Dunn and Hansom, undated west elevation of the 'north country church', *c.* 1873–74. Deep foundations for the cloister and the tower can be seen on the right.

Dunn and Hansom,
'St Gregory's Priory
Church …', drawing
dated 1872.

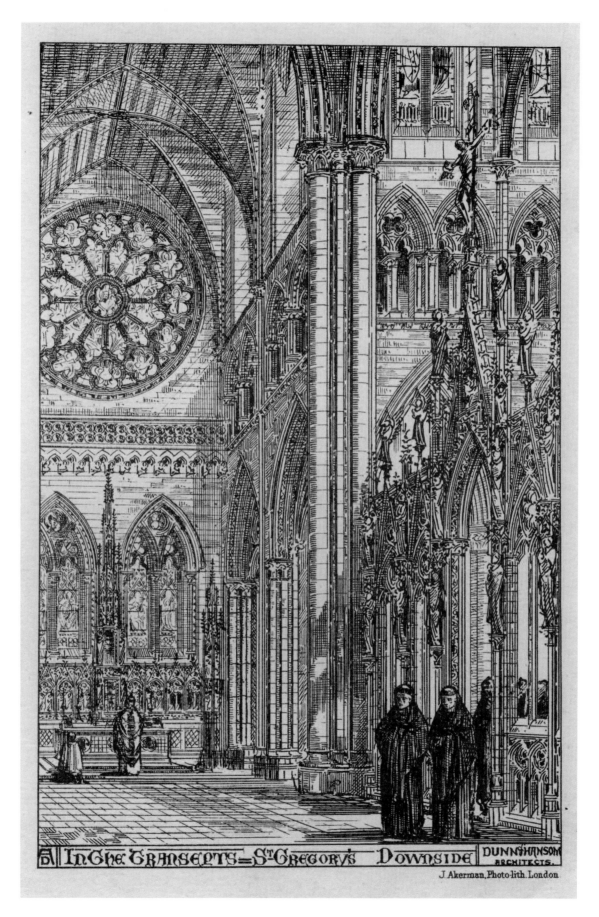

Archibald Dunn, 'In the Transept …', *Downside Review*, April 1881. The rood screen was never built.

'north country' models cited were Brinkburn Priory, Jedburgh Abbey and Glasgow Cathedral.)[24]

The elaboration of a projected sanctuary would seem to follow the letters of November 1879. Northern primitivism has now given way to metropolitan elaboration, specifically in reference to Henry III's choir at Westminster Abbey, with tall, slightly stilted arches with diapered spandrels, paired triforium openings and two-light lancets all now in Geometric forms; two further bays have been pasted on to the drawing of the four-bay choir to make it six bays. The radial apse – another Westminster reference – has behind it an ambulatory, a vestibule and then a three-bay Lady chapel, all vaulted. There is also a corresponding dimensioned pencil drawing with some constructional details showing the use of iron girders.

Then a drawing dated 4 December 1879 takes us back to the standards of the drawings of 1873, with a section through the northern chapels, the choir aisle and the choir showing the apse (p. 105). The cloister aisle is overlaid to show the upper cloister chapels; it should be noted that the easterly chapels are to be straight-ended. This is the last of the drawings showing Dunn and Hansom's choir à la Westminster Abbey, and no further surviving drawings by them are to this standard. Further drawings were sent 'from Clifton', Bristol (where Charles Hansom's office was), 'on Wednesday last' (letter to Gasquet dated 5 April 1880), and Edward makes the weary plea: 'I trust the design as it now stands will meet universal approval – please let me know what is the general verdict.' Tracings were promised from which to work on site, as well as details of all the columns and so forth, so that work could begin immediately. Significantly, no drawings dated 1880 survive, suggesting that any such drawings would have been the ones actually used to build 'Gasquet's church'.

The building of the crossings and adjacent bays (1879–82) is reflected only in such working details as the drawing that omits 'coloured bands' from the transept groining (although that had perhaps already been achieved at lower levels, as in the cloister and St Lawrence's chapel). A letter of 14 January 1882 from Hansom to Gasquet on the groining seems to coincide with this change. An undated sketch plan shows the crossing with single adjacent bays either side in dark ink to indicate construction; the crossing piers are by now strengthened, the isolated north transept pier has gone and the chapels at the north-east end have developed yet further. The building had been started to the extent of measuring the work done against the drawings by the contractor Joseph Blackwell of Bath for 'a complete schedule of the Mason's work', with further measurements given and a change from Ancaster to Roche stone mooted.[25] Writing to Gasquet on 13 December 1880, Dunn claims: 'You know you are doing it very well. There are not many modern churches that have been done so thoroughly … [it] will be worthy of your tradition as a grand building.'

During the final phase before the opening in 1882 there was a flurry of letters and drawings. On 12 February 1881 Hansom wrote to Gasquet to defend a tiled floor by Godwin against cheaper alternatives. In the same letter, sketches by Dunn (who had clearly been on site) of the layout of the choir stalls and benches were criticized by Hansom, who suggested alternatives.

The design of the altar and reredos was naturally much discussed and the length of the altar commented on: Gasquet wanted it to be 11 feet 3 inches (3.4 m) long, but Hansom (also in the letter of 12 February), by comparing it with that at St Dominic's, suggested 10 feet (3 m). 'Detailed drawings to complete the side niches of the reredos' for the mason were sent by Dunn to Gasquet on 16 February, and the drawing entitled 'Lower portion of tabernacle as amended Sept 1881' shows the extent of detail provided.

Details dated 1882 of the organ screen, which divided the church from the cloister, show the

Dunn and Hansom, undated section through nave looking west, 'north country church', c. 1873–74. Only the cloister (left) and monastery (left background) were built. The west end of the church remains incomplete to this day.

architects' riposte to a suggested cast-iron-supported gallery.[26] The richness of the architectural sculpture in the church is explained by the tour to Ely Cathedral, Selby Abbey and Beverley Minster that Dunn and Hansom gave for the sculptor Alfred B. Wall in January 1882 for 'carving of the North transept[,] and as soon as he can get the reredos fixed [Dunn] will come down again to finally determine the carving of it'.[27] The tabernacle was by Hardman, at a cost of £22. 10s. and another £6. 10s. to gild it;[28] it was an off-the-shelf version, since that to Dunn's design was costed at between £35 and £50.[29] Also from Hardman came the great lampidarium beam and its seven hanging lamps, sent on 29 June 1882. All this was to be photographed and then drawn out by Dunn for the *Downside Review*, which also commented on the imminent opening.[30] Interestingly, the drawing recording the dedication of the proposed sixteen altars leaves this dedication as

'Blessed Sacrament'. The altar and reredos, a *chef-d'œuvre* of the taste of the day, surely sum up Gasquet's taste as expressed by Dunn and Hansom and by Wall.

On 21 January 1882 Hansom wrote to Gasquet: 'Our … Reredos is done & John Powell should design the window as a completion of the work'. Glass for the two transept windows had been ordered from John Hardman & Company by 22 February 1882;[31] the company assured Gasquet that the windows 'work out the ideas suggested in your letter',[32] and agreed to reduce the cost from £175 to £150.[33] The templates for the rose window had arrived at Hardman, its cost had been reduced from £350 to £300, and it was to be supplied before the opening.[34] Hansom criticized the glass and seems to have had no hand in its design. His letter to Gasquet of 23 January 1882 instead praises Nathaniel Westlake as a stained-glass designer ('I have no doubt he will give satisfaction'), and

Dunn and Hansom, plan at foundation level, before May 1879, corresponding to pp. 92–93 above.

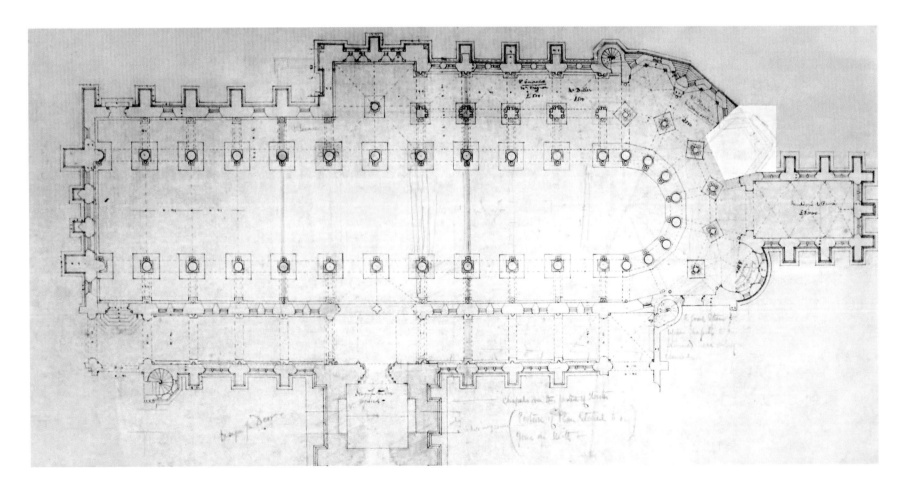

advises on 'groups [of figures] near the eye and single figures high up[;] … any large figures would swamp the groups & delicate work of the reredos'. This is in fact just the advice Hardman followed.

'Gasquet's church' was opened on 11 July 1882. An essential part of its programme was the provision of side chapels, especially those already associated with individual donors.[35] The undated sketch plan mentioned above (see p. 100) shows in red the projected choir, apse and Lady chapel, with the dedications of sixteen altars and chapels in another hand. Most important was the Lady chapel, referred to in Dunn's letter to Gasquet of November 1879, but the details of the crypt were drawn out only in 1885,[36] and the foundations were said to be ready to begin in Hansom's letter to Gasquet of 30 January 1886. Hansom promised Gasquet a plan of the choir and apse to a large scale in a letter dated 25 January 1885, and five days later – still within Gasquet's priorship – proposed a visit to 'settle definitely on the plan of the apsidal chapels'. Here the correspondence, which was begun in 1868, comes to an end, other than an odd letter of 1889 on the window tracery of the Lady chapel.[37] Later drawings are of the chapels, including St Isidore's (1889–90) with its Perpendicular tracery (among other details); the altar and reredos for St Lawrence's (1889); and the altar and gradines for St Vedast's (1890). Gasquet had

achieved his aim of creating a church that his successors would not be able to leave incomplete.

Dunn and Hansom's schemes had their critics, however. The antiquary and well-informed critic Everard Green wrote to Dom Gilbert Dolan to denounce the architects even as the church was begun. His letter of 2 July 1879, written after a visit to Downside, is typical:

> I was sorry to see how you were bound hand and foot to Dunn and Hansom … let Dunn and Hansom build for the Jesuits … as no-one expects good architecture in their houses. When your great church is to be begun … you should ask [John Francis] Bentley [or] Norman Shaw or G. Gilbert Scott (son of the late Sir Gilbert) or Mr Bodley to make your plans. Mr Bentley is I fancy 'miles ahead' of all talent of the day, and (thank God) is a splendid Catholic.

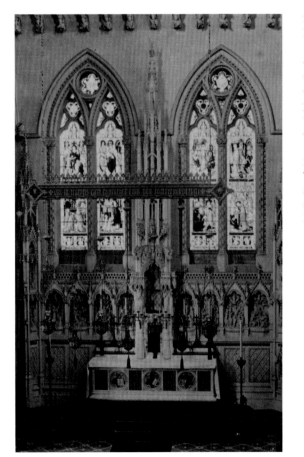

FAR LEFT
Dom Gilbert Dolan (died 1914), one of Gasquet's team of historians, was a constant supporter of an ambitious church, and an active participant, as were many of the community, in the details of design and liturgical use.

LEFT
The north transept, with its highly decorated Dunn and Hansom altar and Exposition throne.

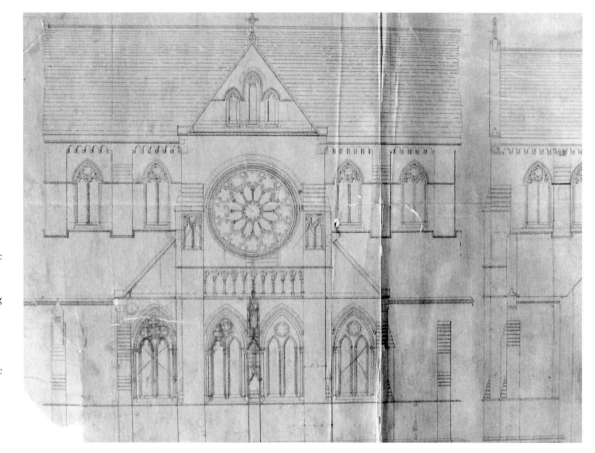

Green and Bentley were both members of the Guild of SS Gregory and Luke, a Catholic artistic study and pressure group modelled on the Belgian Guild of S. Luc (both guilds appealing to Pugin's example). Green was able to work out, influence and establish the complex iconography of the beautiful bosses in the Lady chapel after consulting Frederick Walters and Bentley.[38] Although Green's advice was not taken in 1879, the introduction of Ninian Comper and the appointment of Thomas Garner to build the choir would have pleased him.

Dom Roger Hudleston in the *Downside Review* of 1914 shows an Edwardian disdain for the 'north country' church, which is dismissed as too modest in dimensions (which Hudleston gives) and as foreign in its sources: 'Not in plan alone but in details … the design was wholly French … in the severest manner … in "feeling" far more Cistercian than Benedictine'[39] – the very opposite of the English and 'north country'

claims made by Dunn and Hansom. Hudleston lists Gasquet's changes – the increase of the height of the nave from 52 to 68 feet (from 15.8 to 20.7 m), the insertion of the triforium and the shift from the Transitional to the early Decorated – 'all tending to make the effect richer and more ornate'.[40] Gasquet also added two bays to the choir (originally three, then four and now six bays) and founded a larger Lady chapel (in 1885), which was built in 1888.[41] Dom Augustine James, who, unlike Hudleston (who had evidently not studied the drawings), was more indulgent of what Dunn and Hansom had built (and, unusually for the time, of the Hardman glass), made the curious claim that many – perhaps those familiar with the practice's Cambridge church – did not recognize Downside as being in their style at all.[42]

The architects themselves should have the last word. In his letter to Gasquet of 18 March 1879, Hansom denied that his church was 'Transitional' in

TRANSVERSE SECTION.

(LOOKING EAST.)

'Gasquet's church' is begun: the cloister and base of the tower are shown under construction in *c.* 1881. The techniques of the Victorian builders, and the skill of the masons, reflected a real revival of medieval methods, although Dunn and Hansom were modern and utilitarian in their use of technology.

'Gasquet's church' *c.* 1900, showing the full extent of the Dunn and Hansom building, before the insertion of Garner's choir. The remarkable skyline suggests a work in progress, or even a ruin.

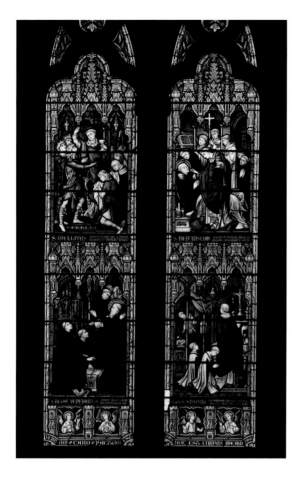

style, having received Gasquet's 'letter and sketches of
the church', which he forwarded to Dunn. Ten days
later, Hansom reported Dunn's views to Gasquet:
"'We must be very careful & very judicious or we shall
have our Abbey Church *ruined* before it was built.'"
On 11 May Hansom wrote to Gasquet:

> I have studied the drawings … and the more
> I think it over the more certain I am we are
> making a mistake in changing a single line of the
> design. We have just got into the trap of having
> designed a building & then trying to *alter it*, a
> much more difficult thing from designing a *new*
> church. You will find that when changes are
> made in a design, they never improve it [citing
> the transepts;] the foundations being in we must
> work with the 14 foot bays … where the
> crossing comes, we should have allowed the
> thickness of the walls extra beyond the bays;

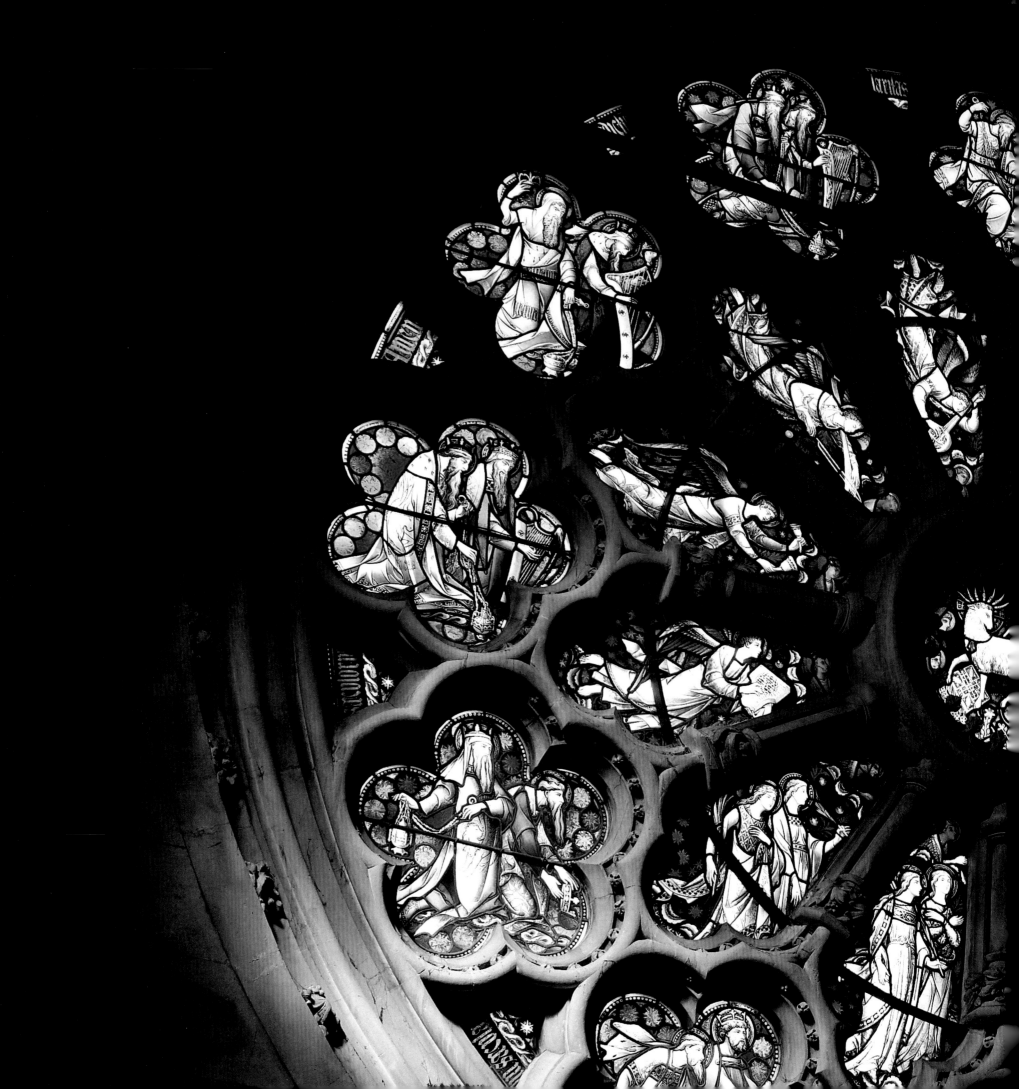

The east end, with Dunn and Hansom's Lady chapel (1885–88) projecting above an open field, suggests a great French church.

now the arches next to the Transepts (E & W) must be constructed to allow for the larger piers.

This last is the reason for the stilted arch in the first choir aisle bay on the north side beyond the transept. On 28 May 1879 Hansom wrote to Gasquet: 'Changes ought not to be made, but if done, the affair should be designed de novo, as a design altered & pulled about is very seldom a success.' The extra height imposed on the scheme, the insertion of the crossing and the larding-over in the Decorated style – all thanks to Gasquet – sacrificed something essential to what Dunn and Hansom had set out to produce: 'An essentially monastic church, [with] a certain amount of severity of moulding and boldness of lines'.[43] In 1895 Hansom's ill health abruptly ended the firm's work at Downside; it would now be the expert task of Garner to reconcile much unsettled business.[44]

1. R. O'Donnell, *The Pugins and the Catholic Midlands*, Birmingham (Archdiocese of Birmingham Historical Commission) and Leominster, Herefordshire (Gracewing) 2002.
2. Pugin's diary, 30 September 1838, in A. Wedgwood, *The Drawings Collection of the Victoria and Albert Museum, A.W.N. Pugin and the Pugin Family*, London (HMSO) 1985, pp. 40 and 81, n. 37.
3. R. Hill, *God's Architect: Pugin and the Building of Romantic Britain*, London (Allen Lane) 2007.
4. R. O'Donnell, 'Pugin's Designs for Downside Abbey', *Burlington Magazine* 123, no. 937 (April 1981), pp. 231–33.
5. A.W.N. Pugin, *The Present State of Ecclesiastical Architecture in England*, London (Charles Dolman) 1843, pp. 105–107,

plate 13; reprinted, with an introduction by R. O'Donnell, Leominster, Herefordshire (Gracewing) 2004.
6. *Ibid.* p. 107.
7. A.W.N. Pugin to Lord Shrewsbury, 25 November 1841 and 13 February 1842, in M. Belcher, ed., *The Collected Letters of A.W.N. Pugin*, I, Oxford (Oxford University Press) 2001, pp. 289–94 and 320–22.
8. Pugin, *The Present State*, pp. 58–59.
9. R. O'Donnell, 'Dunn and Hansom's Church in Cambridge' in N. Rogers, ed., *Catholics in Cambridge*, Leominster, Herefordshire (Gracewing) 2003, pp. 246–55.
10. R. O'Donnell, 'The Pugins and the Belmont Abbey and Monastery' in S. Berry, ed., *The Sesquicentenary of the Benedictines at Belmont Abbey, 1859–2009*, forthcoming.

11. Downside Abbey Archives. A résumé of the correspondence was made by T.E. Muir in 1996.
12. Edward Hansom (hereafter EJH) to Murphy, 24 December 1872.
13. Dunn to Gasquet, 9 January 1882.
14. EJH to Murphy, 4 April 1873.
15. Dunn and Hansom's design for Downside, 1872, in the Downside Abbey Archive, Architectural MSS, Dunn and Hansom Collection, Plate Series. See 'St Gregory's Church and Monastery at Downside near Bath', in A. Graves, *The Royal Academy: A Complete Dictionary of Contributors and their Work from its Foundation in 1769 to 1904*, London (Bell), vol. 2 (1905), p. 389.
16. *Building News*, 36 (13 June 1879), p. 660; *Downside Review* 1 (July 1880), plate at p. 24.

17. EJH to Dom Gregory, September 1873.
18. *Architectural Parallels; Or, the Progress of Ecclesiastical Architecture in England, Through the Twelfth and Thirteenth Centuries, Exhibited in a Series of Parallel Examples, Selected from the Following Abbey Churches: Fountains; Kirkstall; Furness; Roche; Byland; Hexham; Jervaulx; Whitby; Rievaulx; Netley; Bridlington; Tintern; St Mary's, York; Guisborough; Selby; Howden*, London (J. Van Vorst) 1848.
19. EJH to Gasquet, 11 May 1879.
20. EJH to Gasquet, 15 June 1879.
21. EJH to Murphy, 12 May 1873.
22. EJH, postscript in Dunn to Gasquet, 3 November 1879.
23. Dunn to Gasquet, November 1879. The date of this letter is illegible.
24. EJH to Gasquet, 18 March 1879.

The monks' cemetery at the east end of the abbey was opened when the community arrived in 1814, but resembles a war cemetery with its uniform crosses, introduced after the First World War.

25. Dunn to Gasquet, 13 and 17 December 1880. Blackwell was contractor by 1874 (EJH to Murphy, 24 April 1874), and was still in place in 1882 (EJH to Murphy, 6 October 1882); the contractor at the time the foundation stone was laid had been Barnsley of Oulton, Warwickshire.

26. EJH to Gasquet, 4 January 1882.

27. Dunn to Gasquet, 9 January 1882.

28. J.H. Hardman to Gasquet, 4 March 1882.

29. J.H. Hardman to Gasquet, 22 February 1882.

30. EJH to Gasquet, 23 August 1882. See *Downside Review* 1 (July 1882).

31. J.H. Hardman to Gasquet, 22 February 1882.

32. John Hardman & Company to Gasquet, 8 July 1881.

33. John Hardman & Company to Gasquet, 13 February 1881.

34. John Hardman & Company to Gasquet, 4 and 10 March and 29 May 1882.

35. The complicated history and sequence of the side chapels is given in R. Hudleston, 'Buildings', *Downside Review* 33 (1914), pp. 161, 163–65.

36. Dunn to Gasquet, 17 and 25 January 1885.

37. EJH to Dolan, 23 June 1889.

38. Green to Dolan, 26 October 1887; see also Green to Dolan, 1 November 1887, suggesting thirty-one examples.

39. Hudleston, 'Buildings', p. 160.

40. *Ibid.*, p. 161.

41. *Ibid.*, p. 163.

42. *Ibid.*

43. EJH to Gasquet, 26 July 1879.

44. R. O'Donnell, 'Thomas Garner and the Choir of the Abbey Church at Downside', *The Raven* 276 (1994–95), pp. 50–53; and below, pp. 117–51. See also R. O'Donnell, 'Benedictine Building in the Nineteenth Century', in *English Benedictine Congregation History Symposium*, ed. G. Scott, (1983), vol. 3, pp. 38–48.

Thomas Garner and the Choir of Downside Abbey Church

Michael Hall

On 20 September 1905 the Downside community celebrated a pontifical Requiem Mass in the abbey church for the deceased brethren and benefactors of St Gregory's monastery. It was held in the choir, which had been unveiled and blessed the day before. Nothing in the celebrations for the opening of the choir, wrote T. Leo Almond in the *Downside Review*, 'was more impressive than the long file of monks with lighted candles, drawn up on either side of the catafalque at the absolutions, while Faboulier's grandiose *Libera* made supplication for St Gregory's dead'.[1]

The sermon was preached by the Abbot President of the English Congregation of the Order of St Benedict, Dom Aidan Gasquet. He could take particular pleasure in the new choir since it was he who, as prior of Downside from 1878 to 1885, had overseen the beginning of the church with the building of its transept, the lower storeys of the tower and part of the chevet of eastern chapels. Gasquet's sermon reminded the community of the anniversary that was being marked by the completion of the choir, for it was exactly 300 years since St Gregory's had been founded at Douai in Flanders. However, he laid greater stress on what he called the Congregation's *dies memorabilis*, two years later, on 21 November 1607, when Sigebert Buckley, the last survivor of the medieval English Benedictines and a monk of Westminster Abbey, professed during the reign of Mary Tudor, 'gave the habit to two priests, and handed on the rights and privileges of the ancient English Benedictines to us – an act which was afterwards ratified by the Holy See. Today, I am very sure we have all recalled this cherished memory, for it is the glory and boast of us English Benedictines that there never has been with us any breach of continuity with Catholic England.'[2]

Unexceptional as it may sound today, the idea that St Gregory's represented, in Gasquet's words, 'an unbroken Benedictine line to the first Apostle of our race' reflected the new monastic spirit at Downside.[3] Until the 1890s the English Benedictines maintained

The church from the south-east, showing the east wall of the choir designed by Thomas Garner rising above Dunn and Hansom's Lady Chapel. On the left are the square east ends of the chapels of St Isidore and St Benedict and the polygonal chapel of the Sacred Heart.

The choir as completed in 1905. Its lamps, abbatial throne, choir stalls and organ were all subsequently replaced.

the missionary character that was fundamental to St Gregory's when it was founded in 1605, at a time when Catholic worship and monastic life in England were proscribed. The Congregation was organized on centralized lines, on the model of the Jesuits, under the government of the provincials of York and Canterbury, to serve missionary needs. The Benedictine priories that were established in England following the devastation of monasticism on the Continent in the 1790s – at Downside and Ampleforth – had as a result two main roles: to act as seminaries for the supply of priests to parishes and to educate the sons of the Catholic laity. The contemplative, communal nature of traditional Benedictine life was largely secondary. However, once the Catholic hierarchy in England had been restored, in 1850, the notion of the Benedictine order as missionary started to lose its force. A campaign began to restore its monastic life, encouraged implicitly by the establishment of Anglican Benedictine monasteries and explicitly by the foundation in England of reformed Benedictine communities, such as those at St Augustine's Abbey in Ramsgate, Kent (1856), Erdington in Birmingham (1876) and Buckfast in

Devon (1882). However, the abandonment of nearly 300 years of tradition was achieved only with a considerable struggle, and it took direct papal intervention – with the Apostolic Letter '*Religiosus Ordo*' of 1890 – to bring the order of English monks into line. The change was finally instituted by Pope Leo XIII's bull '*Diu Quidem*' in 1899, which instructed the English Benedictines to revise their constitutions on traditional monastic lines. The provincials were abolished, and the three priories of the English order, at Downside, Ampleforth and Douai in Flanders, were raised to the status of abbeys, now in essence self-governing although loosely federated in a Congregation, with abbots elected by their own communities for a period of eight years.[4]

This was a triumph for what had become a 'monastic party' within the English Benedictine order, a party that was to a large degree centred on Downside. Its leaders were Gasquet and his successor as prior, Edmund Ford, who in 1900 was elected Downside's first abbot. Ford made the continuation of Gasquet's work on the monastic church a priority. Building had now reached the point where it was possible to begin

This photograph of the blessing of Dom Christopher Butler as abbot of Downside in 1946 shows the choir in its full glory. Spacious and well appointed, it provided a perfect stage for a theatrical monastic liturgy. The altar furnishings were designed by Giles Gilbert Scott.

the choir. As the setting for the monastic office, the *opus Dei* that St Benedict had stressed lay at the heart of his Rule, a new choir would embody the revived monastic life that '*Diu Quidem*' had brought into being.

Ford was, however, faced with a difficult decision. Archibald M. Dunn and Edward Hansom, the architects of the church to date, had withdrawn from the work in 1895 because of the ill health of Hansom, who died in 1900. In 1898 two architects were employed at Downside: Frederick Walters (1849–1931), who was completing St Isidore's and St Benedict's chapels, and Ninian Comper (1864–1960), who was furnishing the Lady chapel by Dunn and Hansom. If either was considered as a possible designer of the choir there is no evidence of it. No formal announcement of a replacement for Hansom was made, but in March 1900 the *Downside Review* commented that 'Mr Garner has supplied a very interesting drawing for the completion of the tower'.[5]

Thomas Garner (1839–1906) had in fact been in discussion with Ford about the abbey church since the summer of 1898. Ford's well-attested charm concealed a steely will, as had been evident in his leadership of the long-drawn-out campaign to restore traditional Benedictine life in England.[6] 'We owe to him', recorded his successor as abbot, Cuthbert Butler, 'not only the choir, but also the fact that it is Garner's choir; for strange as it may appear now, there was at the time great opposition, and it required all the Abbot's firmness and tact to satisfy the community that Garner should be trusted.'[7] No details of these discussions are known to survive, but, in retrospect at least, it seems evident that Garner's appointment was all but inevitable. Although he had left the Church of England as recently as 1896, he had by 1900 numerous links to the Downside community that must help to explain Ford's decision. In addition, there were almost no Catholic architects available to undertake the commission who could rival his long and distinguished career and undoubted expertise.

Garner, born to a family of Warwickshire gentleman farmers, was a member of an exceptional generation of young Gothic Revival architects trained in George Gilbert Scott's office in the early 1860s.[8] In common with his contemporaries there, notably J.T. Micklethwaite, E.R. Robson and Scott's eldest son, George Gilbert Scott, Jr., Garner reacted strongly against what he felt was the coarseness of mid-century British architecture. The attempt of such architects as G.E. Street, William Butterfield and the young G.F. Bodley to 'develop' Gothic into a style to suit all modern needs, principally by synthesizing native sources with foreign ones, had by the mid-1860s been rejected by all these young men. That reflected the influence not of Scott, Sr., but of Bodley (1827–1907), who had been a pupil in his office in the late 1840s.[9] Family ties – one of Scott's brothers was married to one of Bodley's sisters – meant that Bodley was well known in Scott's office long after he had developed a busy practice of his own. It was thanks to his influence that Scott's young pupils were among the first to employ William Morris's church- and house-decorating firm, founded in 1861, which relied greatly in its early years on commissions from Bodley for stained glass and church decoration. Morris's interest in late medieval English Gothic revolutionized the design of glass, but it also had a much less appreciated impact on architecture. In 1862 Bodley revised his design for a new church in Cambridge (All Saints): foreign influence was entirely erased in favour of purely English forms. Moreover, by 1865 he had abandoned Gothic for his domestic designs in favour of an innovative, and highly influential, vernacular classicism.[10]

Garner was Bodley's faithful follower in both those changes. In about 1863 he set up in practice in Warwickshire, but he failed to find much work, and, following his marriage in 1867, he moved back to London to work as Bodley's assistant. In 1868–69 Bodley suffered a serious illness that left him permanently disabled, prompting him to take Garner into partnership. Garner's reputation has undoubtedly suffered from his thirty-year working relationship with Bodley, who was the public face of the partnership in its dealings with clients, even when designs were wholly by Garner. That may owe something to Garner's natural reticence; he certainly had a less driven personality than Bodley. They differed in other ways, too: Garner was an accomplished draughtsman, whereas Bodley drew very little and had much less strong antiquarian interests. By the late 1870s Bodley and Garner's churches are notable for combining austerity of form with a rich but restrained aestheticism in ornament and colour. These tendencies were well established in Bodley's architecture before his partnership with Garner began, but from 1868 they were brought to maturity in a succession of churches that are undoubtedly the fruit of close collaboration. One of the most significant is St Michael and All Angels in Folkestone, Kent, designed in 1869–70, a building that reformulated the design of urban churches in England. The appeal of English models, so strong in the 1860s, had weakened in parallel with Bodley and Garner's growing impatience with Morris's firm, which was never willing to concede to them control over the design of glass and decoration. St Michael's offered a new synthesis of English and northern European Gothic, in which the simple forms of the thirteenth-century friars' churches of Flanders and Germany were translated into the morphology of fourteenth-century English Gothic.[11] It soon had progeny in the form of the younger George Gilbert Scott's St Agnes in Kennington, London, which opened in 1877.

At St Agnes, however, Scott developed the precedent offered by St Michael, Folkestone, by drawing more emphatically on English late medieval models than either Bodley or Garner would ever do.[12] The Perpendicular style had traditionally been despised by Gothic Revivalists as embodying a period of decline, but to Scott, as to the circle around Morris, it was of particular interest as a distinctively English style. This was not simply a matter of aesthetic preference. Bodley and Garner's churches were undoubtedly based on a deep study of medieval models, but the architects regarded them as essentially modern, designed to serve the contemporary needs of the Church of England. Scott, by contrast, believed that it was meaningless to revive medieval architectural forms without also reviving the liturgy that they had been designed to serve.

St Agnes was intended from the first to accommodate a revival of the Use of Sarum, a form of the liturgy – based on the practice of Salisbury Cathedral – widespread in medieval England. Although there is no evidence that Garner was interested in such ideas, he must have been aware of them. A neighbour in Hampstead of Scott and his wife, he remained their loyal friend and supporter even after their conversion to Roman Catholicism in 1880.[13] Indeed, Garner seems to have been unbothered by such questions of religious allegiance, to judge from Walters's account of their long association, recalled in a letter of 1911: 'I first knew him at least 25 years ago, and did a good deal of work for him before I had much of my own to do. I was much in his society, and although he was not then a Catholic he seemed to like my society because *I was*.'[14]

In 1896 Garner and his wife left the Church of England, as a result of Leo XIII's bull '*Apostolicae Curae*' of that year, which by declaring that Anglican orders were invalid struck at the notion that the Church of England was part of the universal Catholic Church. Although Scott had lost much of his practice as a result of his conversion, it does not seem to have occurred to Garner that he might likewise suffer professionally. However, Bodley was then involved in a prominent commission with a long history of controversy, the provision of sculpture for the high-altar screen in Winchester Cathedral, and there was public criticism of the fact that a firm with a Roman Catholic partner had been employed. As a consequence, Garner decided to sever his links with Bodley.[15] In future, his only commissions from the Church of England were

OVERLEAF
The building of the choir seen from the north. The sacristy has yet to be built. The sloping structure in the foreground was, and remains, 'the stone yard'.

PAGE 123
Seen from the south (Petre) cloister, the choir rises to fill in the gaps. The truncated nave was to be left until after the First World War.

for furnishings in churches that he had designed or restored before his conversion. However, his work for Catholic clients owed a great deal to long-standing friendships with members of the Church of England who had preceded him to Rome.

Among them was a Benedictine monk, Dom Bede Camm, who in his Anglican days had been a curate at St Agnes, where he was deeply influenced by the English medievalism of its architecture and liturgy. These were ideas that he sought to transplant to his new life: in the words of Aidan Bellenger, 'he had a triumphalist vision of the Catholic Church which would make England truly English again'.[16] However, he chose a rather unsympathetic setting in which to realize this ambition, since in 1895 he had joined Erdington Abbey, a daughter house of the abbey of Beuron in Germany, where he had been professed.[17] Most of Erdington's monks were German. Undeterred, in 1896 Camm – who was to become a distinguished martyrologist – commissioned Comper to design a Gothic feretory for the abbey's relic of the skull of one of St Ursula's 11,000 martyred virgins.[18] It seems very likely that in addition Camm was behind the commission for Garner to design a red silk altar frontal of great splendour, depicting English martyrs, and a set of pontifical High Mass vestments, all embroidered by the Sisters of the Poor Child Jesus at Southam, Warwickshire.

Camm also had strong antiquarian and architectural interests, embodied in his best-known book, *Forgotten Shrines: An Account of Some Old Catholic Halls and Families in England, and of Relics and Memorials of the English Martyrs* (1910). He must surely have been involved in discussions about extending or replacing the church at Erdington, designed as a parish church in 1850 by Charles Hansom and by the mid-1890s too small for the community's needs. In 1897 Garner sent designs for a new church to Erdington's Dom John Chapman, also a convert Anglican clergyman. They seem to have been well received, for Garner worked

them up into a set of drawings, now in the archive at Downside.[19] On the scale of a great abbey church, with an eight-bay nave, a three-bay choir and three-bay transepts, it was to have had twin west towers and a crossing tower, all in an English Decorated Gothic style. It was far beyond the community's means, however, and in the event Garner's architectural contribution to Erdington was limited to fitting up the abbot's chapel with a new triptych altarpiece, an oak-and-walnut floor and oak panelling.[20]

Both Chapman and Camm had close links with Downside, which they were to join in 1913 (Chapman became abbot in 1929), and it is surely plausible that Garner's sumptuous scheme for Erdington's abbey church was produced in the knowledge that Downside's new abbot was in search of an architect. Garner may also have realized that Downside would almost certainly be a more sympathetic client than Erdington. Ford himself came from a convert background, and he was welcoming not only to converts but also to Anglicans, as Comper – whose association with Downside lasted from the 1890s to the 1930s – was to find. A former pupil of Bodley and Garner, Comper recalled that he was never made to 'feel an alien there, or that he was among aliens'.[21] Aidan Bellenger has described the change of atmosphere at Downside in the 1890s, as the dominance of the old recusant families was slowly replaced by a broader intake of monks, many of them converts or from a convert background, 'who brought with them much of their Anglo-Catholic devotion to good order and good taste'.[22] It is arguable that their influence went deeper still, and further back.

The desire for a return to traditional Benedictine life was given an intellectual foundation in the historical scholarship that has always been important to the order. After he had resigned as prior at Downside in 1885, owing to ill health, Gasquet devoted himself almost full-time to historical research. In 1888 he published *Henry VIII and the English Monasteries*, an important work of revisionism, as it argued that English monastic life in the early sixteenth century was far from being in a state of decadent near-collapse, as three centuries of Protestant historians had claimed. The book made a deep impression, in part because it opened the way for nineteenth-century Benedictines in England to take pride in claiming that they were a continuation of the monastic culture interrupted but not severed by the Reformation – the belief to which Gasquet alluded in his sermon on the new choir at Downside.

Such ideas owed something to Gasquet's close friend and occasional collaborator Edmund Bishop, the greatest liturgical historian in England. Bishop, who at one time contemplated becoming a monk at Downside, maintained close links with the community throughout his life and warmly supported Ford's reforming mission. Bishop's research had led him to the realization that many significant points in the early development of the liturgy had been of local origin, and were later absorbed into Roman practice, in contrast to the common belief that Rome's liturgical authority had over a period of time simply been imposed on variant native practices. This appreciation of the importance of local traditions was an important factor in his reservations about ultramontane tendencies in English Catholic life.

In 1865, two years before his conversion to Catholicism, Bishop had read A.W.N. Pugin's pamphlet *An Earnest Address on the Establishment of the Hierarchy* (1851), and was deeply struck by its assertion that the Roman Catholics in England had every right to regard themselves as members of a Church, and not a sect.[23] Pugin's pamphlet is now almost forgotten, but it is an important statement of his beliefs as they had evolved towards the end of his life about the relationship between Catholicism and Gothic architecture. He rejected his earlier idea that as part of the campaign to revive Gothic it was necessary also to revive medieval religious and social culture, and turned his back on his old idealization of the Middle Ages: 'Such charity, and such hospitality, and such unity, when

every man was a Catholic. I once believed in this Utopia myself, but when tested by stern facts and history it all melts away like a dream.'[24] Instead, Gothic was to be justified as an embodiment of the fact that Catholicism in England had never died, and had been sustained – and developed – not only by Roman Catholics but also by Anglicans, a notion that got him into trouble with his own Church, as it seemed to imply that Anglican religious orders were valid.[25] It was, however, a view likely to be regarded with sympathy by converts, and it explains why to such an architect as Garner no change was necessary to his understanding of the significance of Gothic when he converted.

Such ideas had, perhaps, particular force at Downside, since the community had commissioned designs for a new monastery and church from Pugin; on which he worked from 1839 to 1842, and although none of his proposals were executed, his drawings were carefully preserved there.[26] Pugin's own practice was in steep decline during the years immediately before his death in 1852, and so it was left to his eldest son and successor, Edward Welby Pugin, to shape his father's ideas into the forms required by contemporary Catholicism. His church plans abandoned reliance on medieval precedent, and employed the shallow chancels that had been the Catholic preference since the sixteenth century, partly because of the Counter-Reformation stress on the visibility of the Mass and partly because of the steady growth of extra-liturgical devotions, most importantly Benediction.

In common with most architects who came to maturity in the 1850s, E.W. Pugin was affected by the fashion for foreign Gothic, and the majority of his churches show strong French influence. It was a manner that by the 1870s, thanks largely to the changes in Anglican Gothic architecture initiated by Bodley, had begun to seem very old-fashioned. In his *History of the Gothic Revival*, published in 1872, C.L. Eastlake condemned modern Catholic Gothic churches – 'Shallow chancels, naves of disproportionate

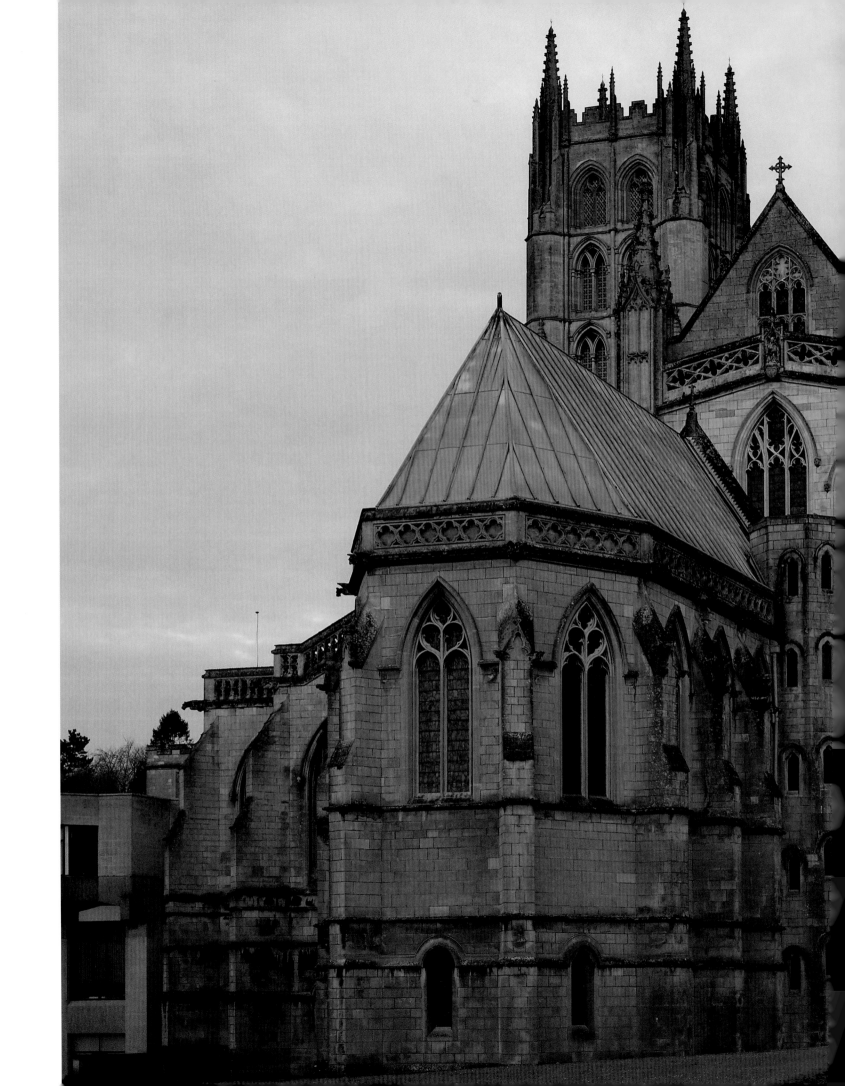

The east end of the church, showing Garner's choir rising above Dunn and Hansom's Lady chapel and radial chapels. The building on the right, which houses the sacristies, was designed by Frederick Walters, and completed in 1915 (see pp. 164 ff.).

width, thin piers, and altars planned after an Italian fashion' – and by then there were plenty of Roman Catholics who agreed, and sought instead to design churches that were distinctively English and medieval in form as well as suitable for modern needs.[27] Dunn and Hansom argued that their first 'north country' scheme for Downside was indeed English.[28]

An important focus for this new approach to architecture and design was provided by the Guild of SS Gregory and Luke, founded in 1879 by Bishop and a group of his friends. Designed to bring together historians, artists and architects in order to encourage new standards in Catholic liturgy and church art, it was firmly Gothic and Anglophile in its interests.[29] Its most important purpose, as Bishop wrote in 1892, was 'to study and know more of the past, more especially of that ancient Church in England, which is ours as Catholics and ours alone'.[30] Its members included the architect J.F. Bentley, who had become a Catholic in 1861, and the painter Philip Westlake, brother of Bentley's close collaborator Nathaniel Westlake, the stained-glass artist. Another significant member was Bishop's most intimate friend, Everard Green, a convert who was to become a loyal supporter of Garner's work at Downside. A close friend also of Bentley (he was best man at his wedding), Green was, in the words of Bishop's biographer, Nigel Abercrombie, 'uncritically devoted to Pugin *et hoc genus omne* and somewhat pugnaciously English in his preferences where the externals of religious practice were concerned'.[31] The Guild never had a journal, but from the mid-1880s it began to publish papers in the *Downside Review*, which had been founded by Gasquet in 1880.[32]

It was not only Downside's architecture that was to benefit from this enthusiasm for claiming the English medieval inheritance for modern Catholicism. In 1896 Richard Terry, another convert and a former choral scholar of King's College, Cambridge, was appointed organist and choirmaster at Downside, and with Ford's strong encouragement inaugurated the renaissance of Tudor polyphonic liturgical music for which he was to become famous. It was at Downside that Byrd's three- and five-part masses were performed as part of the liturgy for the first time since the sixteenth century; Terry also revived works by Tye, Mundy, Morley, Parsons, White and others. 'It is not too much to say', he wrote, 'that the present revival of Tudor music owes its origin mainly to the vision of Abbot Ford and that Downside may be regarded as the cradle of that revival.'[33] Significantly, Terry was keen to stress that this music was essentially Catholic, despite being English, and attacked what he called the 'popular fiction' that such composers as Byrd and Tallis were Anglicans.[34]

The revival of Tudor polyphony was followed by Downside's adoption of medieval plainchant. Here, the key figure was yet another convert member of the community, Dom Alphege Shebbeare, a former member of the Anglican Society of St John the Evangelist (the Cowley Fathers), who in 1904 edited the English Benedictine *Hymnale*. Shebbeare was behind the decision to use the liturgical chant of the Use of Sarum at the opening of Downside's choir, perhaps the first time in a Roman Catholic context in which a revived English medieval musical tradition was performed in a revived English Gothic architectural setting. However, the Downside monks also continued to perform the music they had learned in France a century and more before, such as the late eighteenth-century plainchant of Faboulier, used at the Requiem Mass the day after the choir opened. As T.E. Muir comments, 'given that the basic dimensions of the building were laid down in the late 1870s, it is obvious that the acoustic with its long echo was designed to accommodate the heavier, slower moving[,] measured Mechlin chant'.[35]

In a European context, there were precedents for Downside's combination of a revitalized Benedictine monastic life with modern Gothic architecture and revived medieval forms of music. In some ways it self-consciously looked back to the nineteenth-century reforms instituted by Prosper Guéranger at the Abbey of Solesmes in northern France, where the medieval plainchant revival began, also in the context of a Gothic Revival choir (begun in 1863).[36] One aspect of the Solesmes revival of monastic life could not, however, be precisely paralleled at Downside: Guéranger had been moved to re-establish Benedictine monastic life in France by the sight of the abandoned medieval church at Solesmes, which he restored and enlarged, whereas Downside had been founded on a site without a medieval religious history (in contrast with Buckfast, where from 1883 Walters restored the medieval monastic buildings for the new community). However, the wish by some Roman Catholics to reclaim England's Gothic past in its most tangible form by returning medieval buildings to Catholic use was a significant stage in the path that brought Garner to Downside.

In 1875 Charlotte Boyd, a woman of independent means and strong Anglo-Catholic beliefs, was moved by childhood memories of the ruined abbey at Glastonbury, and the encouragement of the Cowley Fathers, to found the English Abbey Restoration Trust. Its object was 'to provide funds for the purchase of ancient ecclesiastical buildings which had passed into secular hands, and their restoration for worship according to the rites of the Church of England'.[37] In 1893 the Trust acquired the gatehouse and chapel of Malling Abbey in Kent, and handed them over to a community of Anglican Benedictine nuns.

Boyd had been a friend of Camm since his time at St Agnes – he was an honorary curate of the orphanage Boyd maintained in Kilburn, north-west London – and he was almost certainly behind her choice of Garner to restore the next building she acquired for conversion back to religious use, the Slipper Chapel at Houghton St Giles, Norfolk.[38] This small mid-fourteenth-century building, which took its name from the popular belief that pilgrims

left their footwear there on their approach to the shrine at nearby Walsingham, had become part of a farmyard. Boyd bought it in 1896, by which time she had become a Roman Catholic, and so was forced to restore the chapel at her own expense, as the English Abbey Restoration Trust was confined to expenditure on buildings for Anglican use. Garner was commissioned to undertake the work in 1897, and it was largely complete by 1904.[39] At the time of her purchase Boyd had decided to vest the chapel in the care of the Downside community, writing to the Bishop of Northampton in 1895: 'It is old Benedictine ground and I had a great wish to restore it to them.'[40] Although the Bishop's implacable opposition to having a mission at the chapel meant that it did not open for worship until 1934, it was almost certainly, therefore, Boyd – possibly in conjunction with Camm – who first made Ford aware of Garner's work.[41]

Garner is unlikely to have been Ford's first choice if the most significant architect associated with the Guild of SS Gregory and Luke had been available. J.F. Bentley, in such masterpieces as the Church of the Holy Rood in Watford, Hertfordshire (1883–90), had produced for the Catholic Church buildings that fully matched the achievements of the later Gothic Revivalists in the Anglican Church and were wholly English in their forms. However, in 1894 he received the commission to design Westminster Cathedral, making him almost certainly too busy to undertake work at Downside, even if his health had not been in such deep decline by the late 1890s. Ford and Bishop and their circle, who did not have a high opinion of Cardinal Vaughan, Bentley's patron at Westminster, were disappointed by the decision to use an Italo-Byzantine style rather than Gothic (as Bentley himself had initially wished). Although he offered to help Bentley with the planning of the cathedral's high altar, Bishop wrote to Green: 'My own summing up of the building is that it spells … the end of that romanticism which has carried so many of us to "Rome".'[42] Therefore,

The Perpendicular east windows of the square-ended chapels of Saints Isidore and Benedict form a strong contrast with the detailing of the chapel of the Sacred Heart and the Lady chapel, to their right.

although the choice of Gothic for Downside's church had been made when Dunn and Hansom's design was commissioned, the course the building took in the 1890s and 1900s can be seen in some degree as a riposte to the building that was rising at Westminster.[43] Downside's church represented a contrasting romantic, Anglophile vision, in which the liturgical scholarship of Bishop, the ecclesiology of the Guild of SS Gregory and Luke, and something of the nostalgia of Camm's *Forgotten Shrines* were fused with the changes in the abbey's musical life initiated by Terry and Shebbeare. The architectural ideals of Ford and Garner had deep and extensive roots.

Ford had in some way prepared the ground for Garner at Downside in the amendments made to

Dunn and Hansom's design during his priorship (1885–88). The church as originally designed was wholly French in plan, with a chevet of polygonal chapels surrounding an apse. The opening of the Lady chapel, in 1888, was followed a year later by the completion to a new design of the two southern chapels of the chevet, dedicated to St Benedict and St Isidore. They are square-ended, in the English medieval fashion, and their English Perpendicular style is in marked contrast to the thirteenth-century French-flavoured idiom used by Dunn and Hansom in the earlier parts of the building.

This shift is carried through to the furnishings, which also embody the aesthetic preferences of Ford and the Guild of SS Gregory and Luke.[44] St Benedict's was

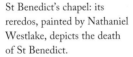

St Benedict's chapel: its reredos, painted by Nathaniel Westlake, depicts the death of St Benedict.

the first chapel in the church to receive a painted reredos, by Nathaniel Westlake; all previous reredos had been sculptural. Its stained glass is by Lavers, Barraud & Westlake, which became from this point the preferred firm at Downside, replacing John Hardman & Company, which had been responsible for the rose window in the transept. Moreover, the reredos in St Isidore's chapel, designed by Walters, is derived from an English antiquarian source, the Warwick Chantry at Tewkesbury Abbey. The significance of these medieval English sources is made apparent by the bosses of the chapel's rib vault, which depict the arms of the English Bendictine monasteries before the Reformation, a statement of the historical tradition with which Ford and his allies intended Downside to be linked.

However, these chapels did not mark a wholesale change in the design of the church. The matching chapels on the north side of the chevet, dedicated to St Joseph and St Vedast, maintain Dunn and Hansom's original plan, although they were completed after the chapels on the south.[45] This suggests that once Ford's priorship ended in 1888 – and from 1889 to 1894 he was away from Downside altogether, in charge of the new Benedictine house parish at Beccles, Suffolk – Hansom simply reverted to his original design. Certainly, Ford's successor as prior, Clement Fowler, who was not a supporter of Ford's mission to restore traditional Benedictine life, seems to have felt no need to continue the change of architectural direction that Ford had instigated.

St Isidore's chapel: an English setting for a Spanish saint.

But with Ford's return as prior in 1894, and from 1898 abbot, the promise of the chapels of St Benedict and St Isidore was amply fulfilled, first in the commissioning of Comper in 1896 to furnish the Lady chapel, and then in 1898 with the approach to Garner, initially about the design of a chapel dedicated to St Sebastian. In a letter to Ford of 22 July 1898, Garner made plain what was really needed: 'I should be very glad to do anything in my power to help you in the matter of the Chapel as I have the greatest desire to do work for the Catholic Church. The work at Downside has suffered much I think from having so many architects employed; and I do not think it would be possible to do a single chapel in a satisfactory manner unless it formed part of a whole which might be realised in future.' There was then a delay of several months, presumably caused by Ford having to persuade the community to accept his choice of architect, but on 23 February 1899 Ford wrote to Garner, 'Would you be prepared to undertake the chapel at once, if a little later you had the completion of the church?' Four days later Garner accepted the offer.

Garner may well have reflected that the changes to the original plan – and the reversion to it – had made his task more difficult in practical terms. In an article published in the *Downside Review* to mark the opening of the choir, he wrote that

> the various chapels which had been added to the building at different times had widely departed from the original style, and it was therefore impossible, even if it had been desirable, to obtain uniformity in this respect in the building. The dimensions, moreover, were rigidly determined. The size and number of the bays, the length and width of the Choir, could not be changed. A symmetrical arrangement was also out of the question, as the chapels on the south side were square at the east end, and those on the north apsidal.[46]

Although there was no precise precedent in his career for the task of completing a substantial new building by another architect, Garner was well prepared for the challenge, since many of Bodley and Garner's restoration projects had involved the sensitive insertion of new elements into old buildings. There are good examples of his skill in such work in churches that Ford may have known, since they are only a few miles from Downside. In 1890 Garner extended the late fourteenth-century chancel at St Julian, Wellow, and in 1891 he replaced an early nineteenth-century south transept and chancel at St Peter, Camerton, a largely Perpendicular church, with a new chapel and chancel. Both works were undertaken by Garner alone, without Bodley. In addition, by the 1890s both he and Bodley were increasingly often called on to bring earlier Victorian churches into line with contemporary ecclesiastical taste with new decoration and furnishings. Surviving examples of such work, as in London at St Barnabas, Pimlico, and St Paul, Knightsbridge, both churches of the 1840s, explain why Micklethwaite once remarked that 'Bodley's the only man I know that can and does make a silk purse out of a sow's ear'.[47]

Nobody would call Dunn and Hansom's work at Downside a 'sow's ear', but the task of knitting together the disparate elements was exacerbated by technical failings. As Garner tactfully put it,

> a difficulty which gave considerable trouble, but which, it may be hoped, is not noticed by the ordinary observer, is the great irregularity of the existing buildings of the church to which the new Choir had to be joined. Probably on account of the piece-meal manner in which the different parts of the church had been built, and the impossibility of getting direct lines through the tarpaulin screens which formed the passages to the various chapels, the setting out of the buildings was

most irregular. No two pillars were opposite each other. The arches had to be different widths, and almost every bay of groining was a fresh problem.[48]

Among Garner's first proposals for Downside was a design for the completion of the tower.[49] To judge from the account of his proposal in the *Downside Review*, his initial ideas differed in some respects from his final drawings for the completion of the church, but in essence they were the same: a pinnacled and battlemented Perpendicular design in keeping with Somerset traditions.[50] Garner envisaged demolishing the existing portions of Dunn and Hansom's tower, an idea that may well have struck Ford as too extravagant; whatever the reason, none of Garner's design was built, and it was left to Giles Gilbert Scott (1880–1960) in 1938 to complete the tower, incorporating the existing lower stages (see pp. 191–93). In any case, the liturgical needs of the community may well have seemed more pressing. Ford had been offered money for a new chapel, and among the first decisions that he and Garner had to make was where it was to be built.

They had a choice between adding a new gallery chapel on the south side of the choir, or building it on the north side, where there was a long gap between Dunn and Hansom's chapels of the Seven Sorrows of Our Lady to the west and St Joseph to the east. There were evident practical advantages to the former position, as the chapel would then form part of the extension of the cloister eastwards that was needed to provide a permanent entry to the church for the monks, one bay west of St Benedict's chapel.

The new chapel was to be paid for by Marc-André Raffalovich, who had agreed to finance it whether it was built on the north or south. Garner produced drawings for the south gallery position, but in the event St Sebastian's chapel was built on the north side, although it was not furnished – by

Comper – until after the First World War. The dedication had been specified by Raffalovich, who had taken the name Sebastian when he joined the tertiary order of the Dominicans following his conversion to Catholicism in 1896 (he was Jewish by birth).[51] In private, Raffalovich saw his new faith as in part an expression of his belief that homosexuals, such as himself, should sublimate their desires in spiritual pursuits. Sebastian had become a familiar *fin-de-siècle* symbol of such ideas, and once the work was under way Raffalovich was eager to understand how Garner proposed to represent the saint in the chapel. Garner wrote to Ford sending a photograph of a painting of St Sebastian, gruffly explaining: 'I looked at the pictures of him in the National Gallery. There are several but this one seemed to me to be the best, and more likely to interest and impress a boy's mind than such a picture as [Francesco] Francia's where the interest lies entirely in the expression. It is by [Antonio] Pollaiuolo.'[52]

In style, St Sebastian's chapel follows English exemplars of around 1400, taking its cue in part from the chapels of St Isidore and St Benedict at Downside. Garner, not surprisingly, seems to have been uncomfortable with the juxtaposition of his work with Dunn and Hansom's. When drawing up designs for the remaining northern chapels he proposed not only amending Dunn and Hansom's design to create a square-ended Holy Cross chapel, matching St Isidore's chapel on the south, but also demolishing the existing polygonal St Joseph's chapel and replacing it with a square-ended building of his own.[53] The result would have been an almost perfectly symmetrical east end, but presumably once again the extravagance of demolishing part of the building – especially one completed barely a decade before – ruled the proposal out. In the event, even the Holy Cross chapel was not built, as it was decided that a space needed to be kept clear to provide access for builders and materials for the construction of the choir.

On the south side of the church, Garner's first task was the completion of Walters's furnishing of St Isidore's chapel. In December 1899 he provided drawings for an alabaster altar and a marble floor using a trefoil pattern derived from the pavement of St Anastasia at Verona.[54] These were executed by the architectural sculptors Farmer & Brindley, always Bodley and Garner's first choice for such work.

In January 1900 Garner began to submit designs for the continuation of the south chancel aisle and cloister in order to link them with the eastern chapels. This took some time to resolve, partly because Garner had to find a way of allowing access up to the gallery chapels, as the existing spiral stair in the tower was too small for the purpose. He achieved it by narrowing the cloister to allow a vaulted staircase, open to the south chancel aisle, to be inserted into the thickness of the wall. Otherwise, Garner's continuation of the cloister eastwards keeps to Dunn and Hansom's design, his only significant change being to omit the striping created by the use of contrasting stones in the rib vault. However, by the time work had begun on the cloister, a far more radical departure from Dunn and Hansom's design for the church was under discussion.

Garner was busy with the drawings for the main vessel of the choir throughout the summer of 1901. On 17 September he wrote to Ford promising the imminent arrival of a perspective drawing. 'The only thing that presses for settlement', he wrote, 'is the question of apse or square end to choir.' Dunn and Hansom had designed a five-sided apse of a familiar French type; Garner and Ford wanted instead a straight east end, which was the customary English medieval preference.[55] Garner's letter sets out the reasons for the change: 'I am quite positive that I cannot produce a satisfactory effect with an apse. Besides other objections there are some peculiar to the present case. The whole scale is too small and there are so many sides to the apse that the windows would be miserably narrow and the pillars crowded together in a way that would be fatal to all grandeur and dignity of effect' (see p. 98).[56]

The main opponent within the community to the idea of a square east end was Dom Gilbert Dolan, whose opinion clearly counted for a great deal, in part perhaps because he had been a loyal supporter of Gasquet and Ford in the campaign to restore traditional monastic life. Moreover, not only had he been closely involved in the choice of Dunn and Hansom and the preparation of their design, but he was also something of an architect manqué – he designed Downside's gasworks – and in 1900 he had made his feelings clear about Garner's proposals for the choir by publishing in the *Downside Review* an article arguing that there was ample precedent for apses in English medieval architecture.[57] At the end of December 1901 Garner had a long meeting with Dolan to discuss the design, and finally, in February 1902, Ford was able to write to Garner: 'We shall have no more trouble about the plans as the decision of our Council last month was final and comprehensive.'[58]

The design adopted, therefore, was for a straight east wall, pierced at arcade level by three arches, in a manner immediately reminiscent of a local model, Wells Cathedral, although the medieval precedent to which Garner explicitly referred in his letters to Ford was Glasgow Cathedral.[59] Above these arches Garner originally proposed a seven-light transomed Perpendicular window, but on 3 January 1902 he wrote to Ford that he had prepared an alternative design, of three transomed windows, 'in the manner of St Alban's, which I shewed Fr Dolan and he seemed to like it much better than the large east window'.[60] The revised design does indeed resemble a Perpendicular reworking of the late thirteenth-century east wall of St Albans Cathedral – significantly, originally a Benedictine abbey church and, like Downside in the modern period, perceived as England's 'premier' abbey – with lancets flanking a

The vault above the chapels of St Benedict and St Isidore (shown here) incorporates the coats of arms of all the pre-Reformation English Benedictine monasteries, linking Downside with its medieval antecedents.

RIGHT
Stained glass by Lavers,
Barraud & Westlake in
St Benedict's chapel.

OPPOSITE
Thomas Garner's choir and
east end with stained glass
by Sir Ninian Comper.

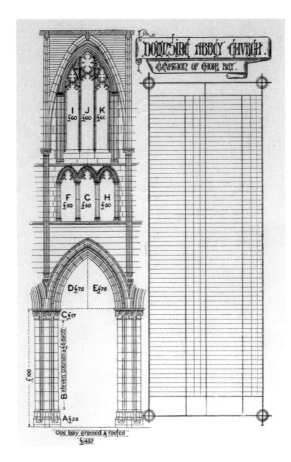

Economic reality determined both the slow building of the church and its developing design. This is a clear and handy guide to the unit costs of an internal bay.

semicircular space behind the chancel's east wall, a space that Garner called the 'feretory'. Ford recalled that the space had originally been intended for Oliver Plunkett's tomb.[62] They were clearly thinking of the arrangement, familiar from many medieval cathedrals, of placing the chief shrine in an elevated position behind the high altar, an arrangement that survives, for example, at Westminster Abbey, where the shrine of Edward the Confessor remains in its medieval position.[63] The problem was that Downside lacked the relics of a saint, although the community hoped that Plunkett, the martyred Archbishop of Armagh, whose remains were brought to the church in 1883, might one day be canonized.[64] In the event, they had to wait until 1975, leaving the 'feretory' without a purpose. Ford proposed, therefore, that it should be floored at the level of the ambulatory rather than that of the choir, so that it could provide more space for processions at the entrance to the Lady chapel, giving it, as Dom Augustine James commented, 'the air of those empty spaces in the eastern parts of the old cathedrals, which have lost the uses for which they were intended'.[65] Garner was, however, able to point to a medieval precedent for the plan, in the thirteenth-century Cistercian abbey church at Hailes in Gloucestershire, now a ruin.[66]

Although the general proportions of the main body of the Downside choir had been set by Dunn and Hansom's and Gasquet's crossing, and the footings for the arcade were already in place, Garner widened the bays, giving the choir a notably lighter and more spacious feel than the transept. At the same time he thickened the walls, allowing him to set the clerestory windows back quite deeply, thus emphasizing in axial views the sheerness of the wall planes, as he (and Bodley) always preferred. He also strove to simplify as much of Dunn and Hansom's detail as possible, eliminating, for example, the ridge rib in the high vault. His first proposals had maintained Dunn and Hansom's three-storey elevation, but in the revised

wider central window above a three-bay arcade. However, the greater width of the choir at St Albans allows for a broad four-light window in contrast to Garner's elegant but rather attenuated three-light one. The revision to the Downside design was criticized by Comper, who argued that the seven-light window 'would have given breadth to the church' and regretted that Garner had 'let himself be over-ruled by the sentiment of imitating the divided east window of St Alban's Abbey'.[61] Judging from Garner's comment to Ford that Dolan had approved the new design, the revision may well have been a trade-off for Dolan dropping his objection to the square east end.

Garner could not entirely eliminate Dunn and Hansom's apse since the ambulatory, which had already partly been built, could not be vaulted without the apse piers. He decided therefore to build these piers up to aisle height. This created a small

The 'feretory' behind the high altar was originally intended for the shrine of Oliver Plunkett, should he be canonized, but that was not to happen until 1975. The Madonna and Child shown here is now in the Old Chapel, where it was banished on the completion of Ninian Comper's refurbishment of the Lady chapel.

design prepared in 1901 the triforium was removed, in favour of lengthened clerestory windows more in keeping with Garner's late-medieval models, such as the nave of Canterbury Cathedral. This change was not popular, as James, writing within living memory of the discussions, makes clear.[67]

Perhaps recognizing that the monks liked the richly sculptural effect of Dunn and Hansom's elevations, Garner prepared an alternative design for the clerestory in September 1901 in which the windows would have been given double tracery, on the model, he says, of Bridlington Priory. This idea was not adopted, however, nor was a proposal by the monks that the triforium be retained for at least the east wall.[68] One other change to Dunn and Hansom's design – the corbelling off of the vaulting shafts just above the arcade piers (in the transept they run down to the bases of the arcade) – was made in order to accommodate choir stalls.

At the last minute, in March 1902, Garner decided to amend his design so that the shafts in the sanctuary were continued down to the ground. There is evidence from other projects that he was inclined to make last-minute changes: at Marlborough College Chapel, for example, designed in 1883, he made a major amendment to the design of the internal elevation when building was already well under way, to the consternation of his client. He was too late at Downside, however, since (as Ford informed him on 16 March) the bases of two columns had already been installed. Garner originally proposed to place the high altar against a screen wall one bay west of the east end, an idea familiar from such medieval precedents as St Albans Cathedral and one that he had earlier suggested for Erdington Abbey, but the community objected that it would not leave enough space for the choir stalls, and so the altar was placed against the east wall.

The final cost of the choir was £16,858. 8s.[69] Building was carried out in the manner successfully established for the completed parts of the church.

Instead of a contractor, direct labour was used, under the control of the clerk of works, Fr Philip Whiteside, a member of the monastic community and the bursar of the abbey school. When the choir opened, Garner paid tribute to Whiteside and to the foreman of the builders and his assistant, 'Mr Brown and Mr Gollege'.[70] It may be significant that Garner says nothing about the architectural carver he had inherited from Dunn and Hansom: Alfred B. Wall of Cheltenham. In his lack of interest in foliage carving, Garner followed Bodley, who had abandoned it at the time of his revised design for All Saints, Cambridge, in 1862. Both men preferred the effect of moulded capitals, which were not only cheaper but also more completely under the control of the architect. An account in the *Downside Review* of the way Garner directed Wall and his assistant, Mr Best, makes clear that they were allowed little deviation from the model capitals and corbels that were produced from Garner's drawings.[71] One of the most prominent figurative commissions, the statue of the Virgin and Child for the exterior of the eastern gable, was given not to Wall but to Farmer & Brindley.

Judging from a letter to Ford on 31 March 1900, in which he wrote that he wished to delay sending drawings for the south gallery chapels until he had had a chance to show them to Green, it seems that Garner consulted the antiquary closely about every stage of the design. In one important element – the arrangement of the high altar – Green (and through him Bishop and the circle associated with the Guild of SS Gregory and Luke) had a significant influence. As early as 1887, Green had written to Dolan: 'My mind's eye saw today the future High Altar, & east end of your choir. The vision I traced to Abbot Islip's mortuary Roll'.[72] He was referring to the celebrated drawing of Abbot John Islip's hearse in front of the high altar of Westminster Abbey in 1532, a unique visual record of the altar arrangements in a great English Benedictine abbey church on the eve of the

Thomas Garner's stairs
to the gallery chapels over
the cloister.

A detail of Alfred B. Wall's foliage carving on the choir capitals. Wall's work was based on models prepared by Garner.

The angel carries the name of Prior Bernard Murphy. The face in the foliage belongs to the Infanta Isabella Clara Eugenia of Spain, founder of St Gregory's at Douai.

Reformation.[73] This image was made familiar to architects and designers by the version redrawn for *The Builder* in 1892 by H.W. Brewer, Bodley and Garner's favourite perspectivist.[74] It was not a model that Garner is likely to have chosen of his own accord. He was happy to follow the precedents formulated in the 1860s by Bodley, who combined altars of essentially modern Catholic form, incorporating a high gradine, with a tall carved or painted altarpiece, often of triptych form, derived from late medieval German or Flemish models. The use of such altarpieces was held up as an ideal by Garner in an article 'On Reredoses' in 1882.[75] Nonetheless, after consulting Bishop, he produced for Downside a design closely modelled on the Islip drawing, with a low retable to be made by his favourite silversmiths, Barkentin & Krall.[76] Above it was to be a tester and, in front of the east window, a rood.

RIGHT
Thomas Garner's tomb in the north choir aisle was designed by Frederick Walters. The Crucifixion at the centre of the tomb is based on a drawing by G.F. Bodley, Garner's distinguished architectural partner.

OPPOSITE
The great clerestory windows of Garner's choir rise above the north choir chapels.

Garner's chief difficulty was adapting the West-minster precedent to modern requirements, for a medieval altar had no place for a Benediction throne. His first idea was to design a niche in the screen behind the high altar, but it was then decided not to have a throne at all, rather placing the monstrance on a removable pedestal on the altar. Garner suggested adapting the hanging pyx depicted in the Islip Roll to form a crown for the monstrance, an odd idea that was – like most of his design – fiercely debated after his death. Very little of what he proposed was executed, and even his design for stone screens to enclose the altar platform was amended by Walters soon after his death.[77] There were apparently practical reasons, in that Garner's design was, according to Walters, faultily measured; his other major change, the replacement of Garner's proposed sacristy on the north side of the church with a much larger design of his own, was necessitated by the requirements of the growing community.[78]

Garner not only left a full set of drawings for the completion of the church, but also made clear his feelings about the choice of craftsmen for the remaining fittings. Butler, newly appointed as abbot, hoped quickly to fill the choir's east window. The obvious candidate to design it was Comper, but, wrote Butler to Walters on 23 October 1907, Garner had not been an admirer of Comper's glass in the Lady chapel:

I am told that Mr Garner more than once expressed himself in the sense that that was not what he wished – that he did not want its 'exaggerated medievalism'. It has these last few days come to light that Garner wished Grylls to do the window & that he had spoken to & given him some idea on the treatment & had actually got him to supply estimate & designs for the windows of the Sacred Heart Chapel.

This is revealing in many ways. Unlike Comper's use of purely English late medieval sources of inspiration, Garner's favourite stained-glass artists, Burlison & Grylls (a firm set up with his encouragement in 1868), blended German and English Gothic forms with figures derived from fifteenth-century northern European engravings and Italian and Netherlandish paintings to create a highly aestheticized synthesis that is quintessentially late Victorian or Edwardian. For all that Garner's emphasis on Englishness helped to transform the abbey church, and reflected the desire of the Benedictine Order and the Roman Catholic Church to be understood not as a mission-ary body but as the historic church of the English people, he was not a medievalist or even an antiquary. He saw himself as essentially a modern architect, serving the needs of the modern church, on the lines set out by A.W.N. Pugin fifty years before.

Garner died on 30 April 1906, having suffered a bronchial attack following a pursuit of a hansom cab in which he had accidentally left a roll of drawings. 'Though ageing and often in poor health, his energy and enthusiasm would have given little suggestion that the end was near', recalled James. 'He is one of our benefactors, for it is recorded that he loved to consider his labours for Downside as a thank-offering for his conversion.'[79] His funeral took place at Downside, and he was buried in the vault beneath his choir, where in 1931 he was joined by his widow, Rose. It was initially proposed that he should be given a monument in St Sebastian's chapel modelled on the tomb that he had designed in 1901 for Arthur Stuckey Lean in the south choir aisle. In the event, however, a more modest memorial was built in the north choir aisle, designed by Walters but incorporating a sculpted relief of the Crucifixion based on a drawing by Bodley.[80]

1. T.L. Almond, 'The Opening of the New Choir', *Downside Review* 24 (1905), p. 262.
2. A. Gasquet, 'The Makers of St Gregory's', *Downside Review* 24 (1905), p. xvii.
3. *Ibid.*
4. For a succinct account of this change, see D. Rees, 'The Benedictine Revival in the Nineteenth Century', in D.H. Farmer, ed., *Benedict's Disciples*, Leominster (F. Wright Books) 1995, pp. 324–49. On the campaign to restore monastic life as seen from the perspective of Downside, see B. Hicks, *Hugh Edmund Ford: First Abbot of Downside*, London and Glasgow (Sands & Co.) 1947, pp. 100–37, which is given a wider context in A. Bellenger, 'The English Benedictines: The Search for a Monastic Identity, 1880–1920', in J. Loades, ed., *Monastic Studies: The Continuity of Tradition*, Bangor, Gwynedd (Headstart History) 1990, pp. 299–321.
5. *Downside Review* 19 (1900), p. 10.
6. There is no modern biographical study of Ford to supplement Hicks, *Hugh Edmund Ford*.
7. C. Butler, 'Abbot Ford', *Downside Review* 49 (1931), p. 13.
8. The biographical sources for Garner are few. The principal obituary is by E. Green, 'In Memoriam Thomas Garner: Artist, Architect and Archaeologist', *Downside Review* 25 (1906), pp. 116–21. See also *The Builder* 90 (1906), pp. 523 and 531; E. Warren, 'Thomas Garner', *Architectural Review* 19 (1906), pp. 275–76; and the revised entry on Garner (by P. Waterhouse) in *The Oxford Dictionary of National Biography*, Oxford (Oxford University Press) 2004.
9. The best published overview of Bodley's career is by D. Verey: 'G.F. Bodley: Climax of the Gothic Revival', in J. Fawcett, ed., *Seven Victorian Architects*, London (Thames & Hudson) 1976, pp. 84–101. See also the entry on Bodley (by M. Hall) in *The Oxford Dictionary of National Biography*.
10. M. Hall, 'The Rise of Refinement: G.F. Bodley's All Saints, Cambridge, and the Return to English Models in Gothic Architecture of the 1860s', *Architectural History* 36 (1993), pp. 103–26.
11. St Michael, Folkestone, was demolished in 1953. It is illustrated in M. Hall, '"A Patriotism in Our Art": Ideas of Englishness in the Architecture of G.F. Bodley', in I. Dungavell and D. Crellin, eds, *Architecture and Englishness, 1880–1914: Papers from the 2003 Annual Symposium of the Society of Architectural Historians of Great Britain*, London (Society of Architectural Historians of Great Britain) 2006, p. 18 (fig. 4).
12. On St Agnes, Kennington, see G. Stamp, *An Architect of Promise: George Gilbert Scott Junior (1839–1897) and the Late Gothic Revival*, Donington, Lincolnshire (Shaun Tyas) 2002, pp. 74–90.
13. Garner remained a friend despite Scott's decline in the 1880s into alcoholism and mental illness: see *ibid.*, p. 327.
14. Frederick Walters to 'Allen', 12 July 1911, Downside Abbey Archives, Architectural History, High Altar.
15. The details of Garner's split with Bodley are, uniquely so far as I am aware, given in 'Odds and Ends', *Downside Review* 25 (1906), pp. 220–22. On the Winchester commission, see G. Brandwood, '"Unlucky Experiments in Statues": Restoring the Winchester Great Screen', *Ecclesiology Today* 31 (May 2003), pp. 3–12.
16. A. Bellenger, 'Dom Bede Camm (1864–1942), Monastic Martyrologist', *Studies in Church History* 30 (1993), p. 381.
17. M. Hodgetts, 'Erdington Abbey, 1850–1876–2001', *English Benedictine Congregation History Symposium* 27 (2001).
18. A. Symondson and S. Bucknall, *Sir Ninian Comper: An Introduction to his Life and Work with a Complete Gazetteer*, Reading (Spire Books) 2006, pp. 57–60.
19. Thomas Garner to Dom John Chapman, 7 July 1897, Downside Abbey Archives, Thomas Garner. The drawings consist of four sheets, showing (1) the north elevation; (2) a longitudinal section; (3) a section looking east with external and internal elevations of one choir bay; and (4) an elevation of the east end and a section of the nave. The drawings on sheet 3 are unfinished, suggesting that discussions did not progress far.
20. B. Camm, *The Church and Abbey of Erdington: A Record of Fifty Years, 1850–1900*, Birmingham (Midland Counties Herald) 1900, p. 42. I am grateful to Peter Howell for this reference.
21. N. Comper, 'Excursus on Downside, Cowley and Sundry Personalities', unpublished typescript, Comper papers (private collection), f. 1. I am grateful to Anthony Symondson S.J. for giving me access to this document.
22. Bellenger, 'The English Benedictines', p. 314.
23. N. Abercrombie, *The Life and Work of Edmund Bishop*, London (Longmans) 1959, p. 75.
24. A.W.N. Pugin, *An Earnest Address on the Establishment of the Hierarchy*, London (C. Dolman), 1851.
25. R. Hill, *God's Architect: Pugin & The Building of Romantic Britain*, London (Allen Lane) 2007, pp. 456–58.
26. R. O'Donnell, 'Pugin's Designs for Downside Abbey', *Burlington Magazine* 123, no. 937 (April 1981), pp. 231–33.
27. C.L. Eastlake, *A History of the Gothic Revival*, London (Longmans, Green & Co.) 1872, p. 347.
28. See pp. 87–115. On the return to English models in Roman Catholic architecture, see R. O'Donnell, 'Roman Catholic Architecture in England: "Irish Occupation" or "Italian Mission"?', in Dungavell and Crellin, *Architecture and Englishness*, pp. 59–71.
29. Abercrombie, *The Life and Work of Edmund Bishop*, pp. 75–79.
30. *Ibid.*, p. 79.
31. *Ibid.*, p. 74. Green (1844–1926), an author on antiquarian and genealogical subjects, was appointed Rouge Dragon Pursuivant of Arms in the College of Heralds in 1893; he became Somerset Herald in 1911. There is

a brief obituary of him in *The Times*, 23 June 1926, p. 18.

32. The Guild of SS Gregory and Luke is mentioned only in passing by Winefride de L'Hôpital in her biography of her father, J.F. Bentley (*Westminster Cathedral and Its Architect*, London: Hutchinson, 1920, pp. 664 and 666). The reason may be, as Abercrombie states (*The Life and Work of Edmund Bishop*, pp. 486–87), that she was 'insufficiently informed'; more likely, she was influenced by Bentley's own dismissal of its importance, as recorded by Abercrombie (*ibid.*, p. 124). Bentley stopped attending meetings in 1885. Nonetheless, the Guild is important as an early focus for many of the ideas that shaped Ford's architectural patronage.

33. Quoted in H. Andrews, *Westminster Retrospect: A Memoir of Sir Richard Terry*, Oxford (Oxford University Press) 1948, p. 35. Terry was master of music at Westminster Cathedral from 1901 to 1924, where the innovations begun at Downside reached a national audience.

34. R. Terry, 'Tallys, Byrde, and Some Popular Fictions', *Downside Review* 19 (1900), pp. 75–81.

35. T.E. Muir, *Roman Catholic Church Music in England, 1791–1914: A Handmaid of the Liturgy?*, Aldershot, Hampshire (Ashgate) 2008, p. 210.

36. A point made by Muir (*ibid.*, p. 210), where he observes that Bishop Hedley's sermon at the opening of the choir 'is a straight summary of the basic philosophy underpinning *L'année liturgique*', Guéranger's theological explication of the monastic office, which had been translated into English as *The Liturgical Year* in 1867. The most important point of difference is that Edmund Bishop and his circle had no great opinion of Guéranger as a liturgical scholar, and distrusted his extreme ultramontanism; see Abercrombie, *The Life and Work of Edmund Bishop*, pp. 272–73.

37. E. Hostler, 'The Charlotte Boyd Connection', in *Walsingham: Pilgrimage and History: Papers Presented at the Centenary Historical Conference, 23–27 March 1998*, Walsingham, Norfolk (R.C. National Shrine) 1999, p. 100.

38. However, it is possible also that she was aware of Bodley and Garner's work through her acquisition of Malling Abbey, as the chapel had been restored by Bodley in 1866, before his partnership with Garner had begun.

39. These dates are based on the correspondence quoted in Hostler, 'The Charlotte Boyd Connection'.

40. *Ibid.*, p. 106.

41. On Downside's links to the Slipper Chapel, see A. Bellenger, 'Walsingham: Downside and the Benedictines', in *Walsingham: Pilgrimage and History*, pp. 117–32.

42. Abercrombie, *The Life and Work of Edmund Bishop*, p. 282. There is no evidence that Bentley took any notice of Bishop's suggestions for the liturgical planning of the cathedral, although, as Abercrombie records, Bishop himself believed that the concept of the baldachin went back to discussions by the Guild of SS Gregory and Luke.

43. The comparison would have been even closer if Vaughan had maintained his original vision of Westminster as a monastic cathedral, served by a Benedictine community; Abercrombie, *The Life and Work of Edmund Bishop*, pp. 235–36.

44. The *Downside Review* 8 of October 1889 describes the chapels of St Benedict and St Isidore as 'due to the late Prior, Dom Edmund Ford': A. James, *The Story of Downside Abbey Church*, Stratton-on-the-Fosse, Somerset (Downside Abbey) 1961, p. 27.

45. *Ibid.*, p. 29.

46. T. Garner, 'A Note on the Downside Choir', *Downside Review* 24 (1905), p. 266.

47. Quoted by E. Warren in 'The Life and Work of George Frederick Bodley', *Journal of the Royal Institute of British Architects*, 3rd series, vol. 17, no. 8 (1910), p. 328.

48. Garner, 'A Note on the Downside Choir', p. 267.

49. Garner writes in a letter to Ford of 13 November 1899 that he has made a design for the tower; Downside Abbey Archives, Garner file.

50. *Downside Review* 19 (1900), p. 287. No drawing associated with this design is known to survive. Garner's final design for the tower is well recorded in drawings at Downside and in the records of the Royal Institute of British Architects. A lost perspective drawing of the design is reproduced in the first edition of *A Guide to the Church of St Gregory the Great, Downside Abbey, near Bath*, Stratton-on-the-Fosse, Somerset (Downside Abbey) 1905.

51. Raffalovich is now best remembered as the close friend and patron of the poet John Gray, the supposed original for Oscar Wilde's Dorian Gray, and later a Catholic priest, but he has a significant place in the early debates on homosexuality through the publication in 1896 of *Uranisme et unisexualité: étude sur différentes manifestations de l'instinct sexuel*. See J. Hull McCormack, *John Gray: Poet, Dandy, Priest*, Hanover, NH (University Press of New England) 1991, pp. 44–48 and 149–50. On the symbolism of St Sebastian at this period, see R.A. Kaye, '"Determined Raptures": St Sebastian and the Victorian Discourse of Decadence', *Victorian Literature and Culture* 27 (1999), pp. 269–303.

52. Thomas Garner to Edmund Ford, 11 February 1901, Downside Abbey Archives (Garner file).

53. The principal evidence for this proposal is a plan for the entire church dated 19 May 1901: Royal Institute of British Architects, Drawings Collection, PA364/1 [4].

54. Thomas Garner to Edmund Ford, 4 and 6 December 1899, Downside Abbey Archives (Garner file).

55. No entirely compelling reason for this long-standing preference of English medieval patrons has ever been identified. The most likely explanation is that a square east end allows a designer to give maximum prominence to the east window, and elaborate window tracery

was a distinctively English medieval tradition. On this question, see P. Draper, *The Formation of English Gothic: Architecture and Identity*, New Haven, Conn., and London (Yale University Press) 2006, pp. 153–54.

56. Thomas Garner to Edmund Ford, 17 September 1901. Downside Abbey Archives (Garner file).

57. G. Dolan, 'The Apse in English Architecture', *Downside Review* 19 (1900), pp. 65–74. On the gasworks, see Abercrombie, *The Life and Work of Edmund Bishop*, p. 122.

58. Edmund Ford to Thomas Garner, 27 February 1902. Downside Abbey Archives (Garner file). On the meeting between Garner and Dolan, see Thomas Garner to Edmund Ford, 27 December 1901.

59. Thomas Garner to Edmund Ford, 3 January 1902. Downside Abbey Archives (Garner file): 'the arrangement of three arches at the east end is very prettily managed at Glasgow Cathedral'. Although there are, in fact, only two arches at the east end of Glasgow Cathedral, the final design of the upper storey at the east end of Downside, in which the windows are in effect grouped into three tall lancets, does in some ways recall the arrangement at Glasgow, in which four lancets rise from the arcade to the roof.

60. The original design is shown in an external elevation of the east end, in the Royal Institute of British Architects, Drawings Collection, PA364/1 [3].

61. Comper, 'Excursus on Downside', f. 3.

62. Edmund Ford to Thomas Garner, 16 March 1902. Downside Abbey Archives (Garner file).

63. At St Albans Abbey the shrine of St Amphibalus was in precisely the location proposed at Downside.

64. As was explained in 'Odds and Ends', *Downside Review* 24 (1905), p. 280.

65. James, *Story of Downside*, p. 54.

66. Garner, 'A Note on the Downside Choir'. The chevet and ambulatory at Hailes were an addition of the 1270s to the originally straight-ended choir built in the 1250s.

67. James, *Story of Downside*, p. 48.

68. Ford tells Garner in a letter of 3 March that the community approves the design of the clerestory windows, but still hopes that 'the triforium will be carried around the east end'. Downside Abbey Archives (Garner file).

69. 'Downside Abbey Church: Circular No. 3, 8 September 1905'. There is a copy of this pamphlet in the Downside Abbey Archives (Church file).

70. Garner, 'A Note on the Downside Choir', p. 267.

71. 'Odds and Ends', *Downside Review* 24 (1905), pp. 232–33.

72. Everard Green to Gilbert Dolan, 1 November 1887. Downside Abbey Archives (High Altar file).

73. The drawing, from the Islip Roll in Westminster Abbey, is illustrated in *Gothic: Art for England 1400–1547*, exhib. cat., ed. R. Marks and P. Williamson, London (Victoria and Albert Museum) 2003, p. 437, fig. 125.

74. *The Builder*, 2 July 1892.

75. *Reports & Papers Read at the Meetings of the Architectural Societies of the Diocese of Lincoln … 16 (1881–82)*, pp. 136–44. See especially Garner's comments at p. 139.

76. Abercrombie, *The Life and Work of Edmund Bishop*, pp. 350–51.

77. Edmund Ford sets out the evolution of the high-altar design in a letter to Abbot Cuthbert Butler, 23 December 1907, Downside Abbey Archives (High Altar file). For the debates about the arrangements for the high altar, see the reports on Garner's design commissioned by Butler from Ninian Comper, Francis Bond and Leonard Stokes, Downside Abbey Archives (High Altar file). There is no evidence that Garner ever discussed the sanctuary arrangements with his old pupil Comper, who was then at work on the Lady chapel.

78. James, *Story of Downside*, pp. 67–68.

79. *Ibid.*, p. 58.

80. *Ibid.*, p. 64.

The Work of Sir Ninian Comper and Frederick Walters

Dom Aidan Bellenger

Sir Ninian Comper (1864–1960), a Scot by birth but not by ancestry, had a long and controversial career as a church architect and designer. He had been articled to G.F. Bodley in 1883, and his early work was deeply influenced by Bodley and Garner, accepting their High Gothic preferences. As Comper deepened his studies in medieval manuscripts he concentrated his scholarly, liturgical and architectural attention on the place of the altar in the church and became, at the same time, an advocate of the revival of the English Perpendicular Gothic of the fifteenth century. In the surviving Perpendicular churches, notably in East Anglia, and in the contemporary Flemish primitive paintings, he discovered an ideal that he attempted to apply to his work across the country. Comper's competence in church furnishing, and his fashionable status, won him many high-profile commissions, including the series of coloured windows of abbots and kings in Westminster Abbey (1909–61). His aesthetic sensitivity and his extensive travels in the Mediterranean led him, in his maturity, to an architectural position that he termed 'unity by inclusion', seeing the Classical as well as the Gothic as part of the continuing great tradition. This was to be given its fullest built expression in the Church of St Mary the Virgin at Wellingborough, Northamptonshire (1904–31), where the black ironwork recalls Comper's work on the Downside Lady chapel gates.[1]

Comper's great advocate was Sir John Betjeman, whom he first met in 1938, and his greatest critic was Nikolaus Pevsner, whose deeply influential *Buildings of England* series variously derides his work or ignores it. Concerning St Cyprian's Clarence Gate, in London, wrote Pevsner, 'there is no reason for the excesses of praise lavished on Comper's church furnishings by those who confound aesthetic with religious emotions'. This comment was omitted in the new edition of 1991.[2]

Comper, whose scholarly adherence to fine materials and excellent craftsmanship was combined with a testy personality, was deeply influential on the 'atmosphere' and liturgical arrangements of the

✠ DOMINVS ✠ DEVS ✠ ISRAEL ✠   ✠ INGRESSVS ✠ EST ✠ PER ✠ EAM ✠

Anglo-Catholic wing of the Church of England, not least in his long-term advocacy of the 'English altar' with its riddle posts and curtains. He was an expensive architect, always wanting the best materials and the finest fabrics, a designer for the luxury end of the market. Only at Downside did he have a significant impact on the taste and sensibility of the English Roman Catholic community. There he demonstrated, in collaboration with the community, that it was possible to marry Roman Catholic and English liturgical design in a creative and arresting way. His impact on the character of Downside's abbey church would be crucial.

Comper's work at Downside began in 1896 and continued until 1951. According to his biographer, Anthony Symondson, who has transformed our knowledge of the architect, the abbey church contains some of his best work, and charts the evolution of his style. His work at Downside is far-reaching and influential, but is more about furnishing than about stones or bricks and mortar. Despite his enormous visual impact on the place, he was not responsible for the design of any new part of the building.

Comper's commissions at Downside owe their origins to the Anglo-Catholic clergyman Arthur Stapylton Barnes, who was resident there after his reception into the Church. The altar for the Lady chapel was presented by Barnes in thanksgiving for his conversion. It was constructed on a monumental scale quite different in quality and liturgical nuance from the altars of the Dunn and Hansom chapels, which are dominated by gradines. In the Lady chapel the stone altar table was enclosed by four riddle posts of wrought iron topped by taper-bearing angels with hangings. The east end of the apsidal space was squared off to form a small sacristy approached by two oak doors.

The first phase of the scheme was complete by 1898. It pleased the eirenic Comper that this was 'one of the first unchallenged acceptances of "the English Altar"', and that every new altar in the great church was designed 'in conformity with it … an important witness to a fact which is far too much forgotten, viz., that between what is really English and really Roman there is no difference'.[3]

In 1913 the altar was completed with the addition of new riddle posts, a new retable (or reredos), relic chests and a crucifix. The east wall was decorated in blue and gold. The five panels of the retable represent the Christ-Child with Our Lady and St Anne, between representations of the Nativity, the Adoration of the Magi, the Presentation in the Temple and the traditional appearance of Jesus to his mother after the resurrection – all framed within the allegorical 'stem of Jesse'. In the lower right-hand corner are the arms of the donor, General Sir William Butler, who presented the retable to commemorate the priestly ordination of his son Dom Urban Butler. The four gilt arks contain the skull of St Thomas of Hereford and relics of St Maurice, St Aidan of Lindisfarne and St Olympias. The tester hanging over the altar depicts the coronation of the Virgin Mary, and at each corner are the arms of the ancient West Country abbeys dedicated to the Virgin: Glastonbury, Tewkesbury, Milton and Sherborne. The altar frontal has black orphreys, which refer to the text from the Song of Songs.

The alabaster carvings of the retable, richly decorated in gold, reflected the influential Nottingham alabaster school of sculptors, whose work is found across Europe. Their work represents a lost Catholic world of the late Middle Ages, delightfully recaptured by Comper. For Anthony Symondson, it is 'one of the first works of religious art of the earliest twentieth century'. Comper wanted to complete the decoration of the Lady chapel by painting the stonework with diaper patterns and the groined vault (its bosses already carved with representations of flowers and herbs associated with Our Lady) with gold and a firmament of stars.[4] This was never achieved, but the flight of stairs, the gilded statue of the Virgin – modelled, it is said, on Comper's wife – under a crocketed canopy (designed in 1915) and the iron gates were installed in 1929.

Comper's transformation of the Lady chapel included a resplendent English altar, relic 'arks', stained glass and painted tester.

The Christ-Child with his mother and his grandmother, St Anne, at the centre of the Comper retable (right). The Magi present their gifts (far right). The retable is resplendent with gold and rich colours.

The stained-glass windows of the Lady chapel, also by Comper, were put in place gradually over a period of twenty-seven years from 1899, and some of them are memorials to pupils killed in the First World War or who died in the school. The east window, depicting the Annunciation, came first, and all the windows, which form a meditation on the Virgin's life, reflect Comper's late medieval inspiration with an emphasis on light, forming a contrast to the opaque heaviness of much of Downside's Victorian glass. The windows were not to everyone's taste, but the archaeologist architect Francis Bligh Bond – who was not noted for understatement – declared them 'easily the best modern glass in England'.[5] The chapel of the Sacred Heart, at the south-west end of the Lady chapel, has Comper's most colourful windows, completed in 1914 and in marked colour contrast to his designs for the Lady chapel.

Comper's work continued outside the Lady chapel. A beardless and youthful statue of St Benedict was placed in the chapel dedicated to the saint in 1919. The exuberant reredos in St Sebastian's chapel, complete by 1929, has a central figure in alabaster depicting the martyr between panels representing St George slaying the dragon (on the left) and St Nicholas of Myra, flanked by two smaller figures of SS Cosmas and Damian.

Comper's final work, which dominates the church, is the east window of the choir, inserted when Sir Giles Gilbert Scott's nave was completed in 1936. The window, with its figures standing out boldly against the vivid blues of its background, represents the glory of Christ in His Mystical Body. It is a parallel composition to that in the Lady chapel with the figure of Jesse at the base, the human root from which grows a stem that bursts into flower in the Blessed Virgin and gives birth to the Incarnation of God. The dominating figure of Christ shows him as a young man. In the inclusive work of this latter part

A beardless St Benedict by
Comper, near Gasquet's
tomb.

of his career Comper was significantly influenced by the melange of Sicilian art, which combined the Byzantine, Romanesque, Saracenic and Baroque. The oversized Christ in Majesty owes little to the Gothic Revival and much to the architecture of Palermo. It points, too, somewhat to the Christ in Majesty designed by Graham Sutherland for Basil Spence's new cathedral in Coventry (1962). The whole composition acts as a reredos or even a theatrical backdrop to the sanctuary below.

Advocates of Scott's 'purism', who regarded Comper as somewhat decadent, did not take to the great east window. Dom Anselm Rutherford, the great supporter of Scott, who commissioned Scott's early Christian church of St Alphege in Bath, described it as 'a tragedy', reflecting the high feelings generated by the work that effactully completed the abbey church.[6] These feelings were reflections, too, of the liturgical archaeology that began in the first half of the twentieth century to question the assumptions

of the Counter-Reformation and even medieval Revivalism. Comper's plan for the completion of the sanctuary, proposed in the late 1920s, was a free-standing altar at the west end of the choir crowned by a high gilded ciborium of Classical design, with the choir stalls behind it. This was too revolutionary at that time even for the most forward-looking members of the community, but Comper's ground plan – minus the ciborium – is what was finally executed in 1968 by Francis Pollen, and remains in place. Influential, too, on the Downside aesthetic were Comper's frontals and vestments; the characteristic Gothic cut of his chasubles, in particular, is reflected still in nearly all the chasubles used in the church.

There remains some uncertainty about Comper's reputation. He 'may or may not have been the most impressive British church architect of the twentieth century', writes Timothy Mowl, 'but he was certainly the most gloriously high camp.'[7] At Downside accusations of pastiche and mere copying seem less

St George and the dragon (right) and St Nicholas of Myra resurrecting the three pickled children from the barrel (far right) flank the central figure (opposite) on the altar of St Sebastian's chapel.

The alabaster St Sebastian is
surrounded by heraldic
angels, the arrows making
little obvious impact.

Comper's design for
St Sebastian's chapel.

St Sebastian's chapel with its fine fifteenth-century Italian primitive painting on wood on the northern (left-hand) wall. The art historian Kenneth Clark attributed the painting to Francesco Botticini (1446/47–1498). The screen to the south was completed in the 1970s. In the foreground is the tomb of a member of the Van Cutsem family, benefactors of the chapel.

persuasive than the pure visual delight of his designs, which capture something of the ethic he advocated.

The Downside sacristy is probably the largest building of its kind in England, and with its splendid wooden furnishings fulfils its function admirably. Its Perpendicular style is not inspiring, however, and to many its conventional details are the least satisfactory part of the whole building. Frederick Walters (1849–1931) designed the sacristy and its hidden chapel of St Conrad (named after

Downside monk Dom Conrad Banckaert, who died in 1910, whose fund-raising made the building possible, and whose emblematic spider is memorialized in the building).

Walters first appeared on the Downside architectural horizon in 1896 with his furnishing of the chapel of St Benedict, its English alabaster altar dominated by the large painted triptych by Nathaniel Westlake with central panel showing the death of St Benedict (see p. 132). Westlake was also used by

The highly decorated reredos of the Oliver Plunkett chapel. The frontal, 'the Alleluia Antependium', used only in Paschaltide, was originally destined for Erdington Abbey in Birmingham, and was commissioned by John Camm, Dom Bede Camm's father. Made and embroidered by the Sisters of the Poor Child Jesus in Southam, Warwickshire, it arrived in 1914.

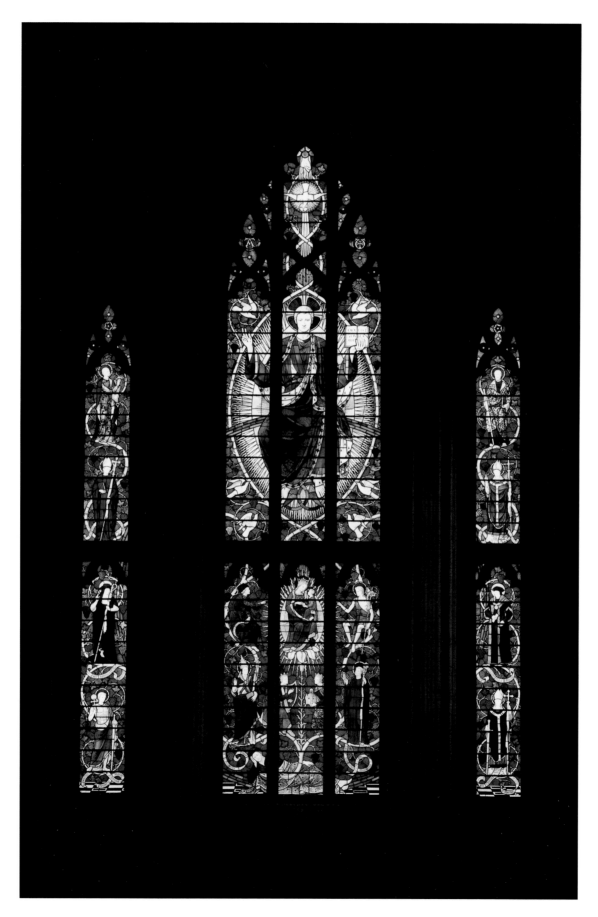

LEFT
Comper's great east window
is dominated by the seated
figure of Christ.

OVERLEAF
The sacristy on the north side
joins Garner's choir to the
copper-roofed chapels of the
Dunn and Hansom church.

Frederick Walters's original pencil-and-watercolour drawing for the tomb of Bishop Charles Walmesley, Vicar Apostolic of the Western District 1770–97.

Walters to paint the doors of the large reliquary cupboard in St Lawrence's chapel. Walters's hand is present in many other details of the church, including most of the tombs, and in the completion of Thomas Garner's work in the choir.[8]

Walters was much used by the Roman Catholic Church and by the Benedictines in particular. His largest church was Buckfast Abbey, first sketched in 1885 and started in 1907; it is roughly contemporary with Garner's work at Downside. Built on the site of its medieval predecessor, it was given 'a painstaking Transitional Norman' style by Walters; as with his work at Downside, 'the fittings are in their way more exciting than the architecture'.[9] For Ealing, then a dependency of Downside, he designed in 1890 a large Perpendicular church with flushwork of an East Anglian type, a style he also used in the Jesuit church at Wimbledon; and it was to the Perpendicular that he returned when designing the Downside sacristy, which opened in 1915.[10]

The sacristy forms a suite of three rooms: a working sacristy, a robing area for choristers and altar servers, and the priests' sacristy, a fine formal space. 'Its lofty timbered roof', Dom Augustine James tells us, 'with wall posts resting on corbels, its range of Perpendicular windows and the linen pattern oak work of its vestment cupboards and vesting benches give an air of Tudor spaciousness.'[11] The altars of the abbey church each have their own vesting bench, not dissimilar to horseboxes, with drawers containing the vestments in the various liturgical colours; the high-altar vesting bench at the eastern end of the building, with its carved triptych, almost appears like an altar. The piscina at the western end, with a monumental tap, has a canopied carving reflecting an alabaster representation of the Annunciation at Wells Cathedral. The oak work throughout the sacristy was designed by Walters himself, but extended, according to Banckaert's notes, by M. de Wispelaere of Bruges.

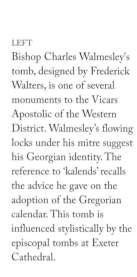

LEFT
Bishop Charles Walmesley's tomb, designed by Frederick Walters, is one of several monuments to the Vicars Apostolic of the Western District. Walmesley's flowing locks under his mitre suggest his Georgian identity. The reference to 'kalends' recalls the advice he gave on the adoption of the Gregorian calendar. This tomb is influenced stylistically by the episcopal tombs at Exeter Cathedral.

OVERLEAF
The vesting benches are laid out for Mass. Each bench corresponds to an altar in the church and contains a set of drawers holding vestments in the different liturgical colours.

English

Canon One

Tomorrow
Festal White
White
Red
Green
Purple
Black
Blue
Rose

The sacristy cupboard, on the north and south wall, contains vestments for special occasions, including the Moriarty chasuble, made at Stanbrook Abbey in Yorkshire.

The splendid fittings of the church, and their craftsmanship and quality, reflect a great collaborative effort made possible by the genius of the Benedictine spirit. It may be unfortunate that few decorative schemes – including Comper's – were fully completed, but this adds to the interest of the building as it now stands, and to its sense of creative edge.

When Giles Gilbert Scott's design for the nave of the abbey church was realized in 1925 (see pp. 177–99), it quickly became apparent that the existing organ, by Garrard, Spooner and Amphlett (1907), was not suitable for so large a building. In 1929 an order was placed with the John Compton Organ Company, a firm that – although well-known for cinema and concert-

hall organs – was keen to break into the market for large ecclesiastical instruments. The new instrument for Downside Abbey Church was designed by Compton and J.I. Taylor and completed in 1931, and incorporated some of the old Garrard pipework.

The inaugural recital was given on 12 February by the organist of St Eustache, Paris, Joseph Bonnet, who was 'absolutely delighted' with the new instrument. 'The tone is marvellous in its nobility, grandeur and charm,' he added. 'This instrument possesses an infinite variety of tone colour.' Other eminent organists were equally thrilled: Sir Walter Alcock found 'the voicing in every department … perfect', and for Sir Richard Terry the tone was

The vestment press at the east end of the sacristy is for the principal celebrant at Mass. The processional cross is thought to be sixteenth-century French. The Deposition, which dates from the eighteenth century, is probably the only painting from Old Douai at Downside.

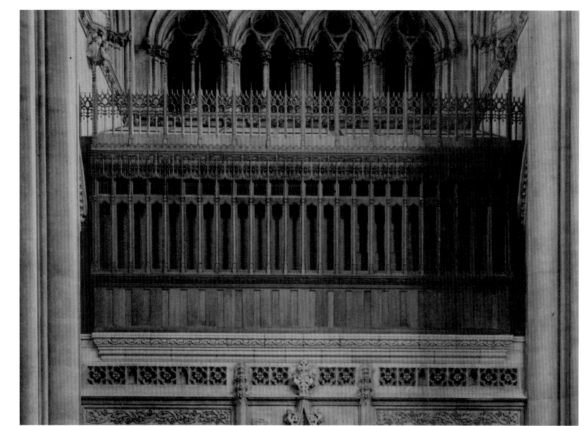

RIGHT, TOP
The solid oak organ screen, designed by Sir Giles Gilbert Scott, was put in place in 1931, after the inaugural recital. It has no roof, allowing the sound to carry up into the vaults and down the nave.

RIGHT, BOTTOM
The console faces west, its four manuals inclined towards the player. The original luminous stop-touches are laid out on sloping jambs in rows of three in each division.

'perfectly beautiful, both in the individual stops and in the building up of combinations'.

The console is on the north side of the transept at the crossing, and contains a number of features that were innovative at the time. The four manuals incline progressively towards the player, and the stops are arranged on both sides of the manuals on oblique stop jambs. The case, which was designed by Scott, is of oak, and the music desk and stop jambs are of teak from HMS *Bellerophon*, the ship that carried Napoleon after the battle of Waterloo.

The Compton organ at Downside was the first to be built with luminous disc stop controls, which Compton had invented in 1917. The stop is 'on' when the disc is illuminated, and each knob incorporates a cancelling action to turn off the other stops in that division. (When the console was rewired in 1992, the cancellers were connected to a switch, enabling them to be turned off entirely, if required.) The light bulbs

for the indicators have now been discontinued, and have to be made by hand.

Two of the manuals have a second-touch mechanism, enabling two stops to be selected simultaneously depending on the pressure on the keys. There are sustainers on the choir and solo, and a pedal-to-choir coupler. Ventil switches underneath the stop-jambs on either side of the console allow each rank to be isolated in case of ciphering or other faults. The rewiring of 1992 added eight general pistons and eight lockable capture memories.

The organ itself is completely enclosed and stands on the gallery at the south of the transept. The screen, designed by Scott and carved by Ferdinand Stüflesser, was not installed until after the first recital. Three chambers contain thirty-one ranks of pipes, each on its own wind chest and with separately controlled wind pressure, and arranged in such an order as to allow easy access for tuning.

1. A. Symondson, 'Sir (John) Ninian Comper', in *The Oxford Dictionary of National Biography*, Oxford (Oxford University Press) 2004, vol. 12, pp. 873–77.
2. N. Pevsner, *London Except the Cities of London and Westminster*, London and Harmondsworth (Penguin) 1952, p. 329; see T. Mowl, *Stylistic Cold Wars: Betjeman Versus Pevsner*, London (John Murray) 2000.
3. N. Comper, *Further Thoughts on the English Altar, or Practical Considerations on the Planning of a Modern Church*, Cambridge (W. Heffer and Sons) 1933, p. 30.
4. Comper to Abbot Leander Ramsay, 4 November 1926.
5. A. Symondson and S. Bucknall, *Sir Ninian Comper: An Introduction to his Life and Work*,
Reading, Berkshire (Spire Books) 2006, p. 50.
6. A. James, *The Story of Downside Abbey Church*, Stratton-on-the-Fosse, Somerset (Downside Abbey) 1961, p. 96.
7. Mowl, *Stylistic Cold Wars*, p. 126.
8. See A. James, *The Story of Downside Abbey Church*, Stratton-on-the-Fosse, Somerset (Downside Abbey) 1961, *passim*.
9. B. Little, *Catholic Churches Since 1623*, London (R. Hale) 1966, p. 181.
10. *Ibid.*, p. 178.
11. James, *Story of Downside*, p. 69.

The organ pipes before the installation of Scott's screen. The pipes are arranged in three stone-and-concrete chambers, as follows:

Chamber A (containing pipes of the Great and Choir organs)
1. Posaune
2. Tromba
3. Diapason I
4. Diapason II
5. Diapason III
6. Diapason IV
7. Salicional
8. Hohl Flute
9. Flauto Traverso
20. Clarinet
21. Tierce
22. Gedeckt
23. Dulciana
24. Vox angelica
25. Celeste
26. Gemshorn
30. Diaphone

Chamber B (containing pipes of the Swell and Solo organs)
10. Trumpet
11. Hautboy
12. Horn
13. Gamba
14. Geigen
15. Strings II ranks
16. Violone
17. Diapason
18. Stopped Diapason
19. Harmonic Flute
28. Harmonics IV
29. Oboe
31. Great Flute

Chamber C
27. Tuba

Downside Abbey and
Sir Giles Gilbert Scott

Gavin Stamp

The present magnificence of Downside Abbey Church owes much to the architect Sir Giles Gilbert Scott (1880–1960), for it was he who was responsible for the long nave that balances the choir, as well as for heightening and improving the tower and designing several tomb monuments and other furnishings. And, had the funds been available, he would have completed this great Gothic Revival building, for, shortly before the Second World War, he also produced a design for the unfinished west end of the church. 'The question I put to myself', Scott wrote to Abbot Cuthbert Butler in 1918, soon after being asked to design the nave, 'was shall I attempt to do something finer than the Choir or shall I content myself with merely carrying on the Choir design? The latter course was the easier and would save a lot of trouble and the result would be safe, though dull.'[1] In the event, he was obliged to continue the essential form of the earlier transepts and choir, so adding to the consistently harmonious character of the slowly evolving church, but in Scott's hands Gothic was never dull.

Scott accepted the invitation to build the nave in September 1917. At that time the Third Battle of Ypres was drawing to its miserable conclusion at Passchendaele, and the new nave was intended as a memorial to the Downside boys who had died – and would yet die – in the war. Scott was an obvious choice as architect. Known as the designer of the great Anglican cathedral that was rising in Liverpool, he had been brought up a Roman Catholic and was responsible for several distinguished Catholic churches designed before the war, at Bournemouth, Sheringham in Norfolk, Northfleet in Kent and Ramsey on the Isle of Man. But this commission was not, in fact, his first contact with the monks and abbot of Downside.

In 1906 a ruinous fifteenth-century tithe barn, the oldest building in the nearby town of Midsomer

The north aisle, with Scott's soaring lines, terminates in an inadequate porch at the temporary west end. The candles are on the consecration crosses. Unusually for a Catholic church, there are no Stations of the Cross.

Scott's conversion of the
barn in Midsomer Norton
retained the medieval
roof and incorporated the
Georgian tabernacle formerly
in the Church of Our Lady
of the Assumption and
St Gregory (known as the
Bavarian Chapel), Warwick
Street, London.

Norton, had been secretly bought by Downside Abbey for use as a Roman Catholic church. Nothing was done with it for a few years, but in 1911 Scott was asked to look at the structure. 'I think the barn lends itself very well to the purpose of converting it into a church', he reported. 'I do not at all feel that it is too much of the "barn" type for the purpose … In the matter of interest the barn is certainly worth preserving, &, at present, is not too dilapidated.' His estimate of £1600 was, however, considered by Butler 'an enormous figure … It will be a serious question whether it would not be better from a religious point of view to allow the barn to its fate & put up a frankly non-architectural structure, even in eternite, for a third of the money. I have little sympathy with expensive architecture in places like Norton.'[2] Dom Roger Hudleston argued strongly in favour of using the barn, however, and the conversion work was finally authorized in August 1912. The ancient building was carefully repaired and the interior whitewashed and simply furnished, all for some £1100. Shortly before the Church of the Holy Ghost in Midsomer Norton was consecrated in May 1913, Butler wrote to Scott: 'I went down the other day & was exceedingly pleased with all you have done: it will gradually be turned into an admirable permanent church of singular interest & I am sure of great beauty too.'[3]

It is scarcely surprising, therefore, that Scott was the architect whom Butler approached four years later. By the end of that terrible year, 1917, he had produced a design for the nave, which he estimated at some £25,000 to build. He had also been asked to consider a separate boys' chapel, and this he proposed should be constructed as a continuation of the north transept. As regards the nave, Scott explained to Butler that 'I have adopted a very large clerestory and small aisles in order to produce a more striking and original effect than can be obtained by keeping the aisles and clerestory of about the same height[,] as is done in the choir. I think the choir bays are also too narrow producing a cramped effect, especially outside[;] the nave bays I have made larger.' Unfortunately, this scheme was not well received. 'To be frank,' replied Butler, 'we were rather startled, it is so different from what we had expected.'[4]

Two months later, in March 1918, Scott sent to Downside an alternative design, which he considered better than his first; it was also more expensive, as the aisles were to be 'considerably higher'. He explained that 'by reducing the thickness of the cloister wall to two feet [60 cm] and thus bringing it in line with the wall of the monastery, the south aisle becomes practically the same width as the north aisle and gives ample width for processional purposes.'[5] Both designs, unfortunately, now seem to be lost. Dom Augustine James recorded that he was told that Scott's 'original plan contemplated a nave of enormous arches, without triforium or clerestory, reaching nearly to the vaulting, and side aisles so low as to be little more than passages'.[6]

However, while terrible battles raged on the other side of the English Channel after the Germans launched their final offensive on the Western Front, the monks came to the conclusion that Scott's proposals were, as James put it, 'in too violent contrast with the style and proportions of the existing parts of the church', and that the new nave should follow the lines of Thomas Garner's choir.[7] Scott wrote to the abbot on 26 April 1918 to explain what lay behind his design, and the letter is worth quoting at length, as it is revealing about his attitude to medieval precedents as well as his approach to architecture:

As I understand that some of the Council are in favour of carrying the Choir design into the Nave, I think it would be well for me to put a few points before the Council for their consideration, which will I hope help them to take a broad view of this very important question.

In the first place let me say that I welcome any criticisms or opinions. These are often helpful or can be met without sacrifice of essentials, but I hope that the Council will not, in their own interests[,] change their original intention, as I was given to understand it, viz. of allowing their Architect a free hand in matters purely aesthetic.

As regards the nave design, I gave this a great deal of thought before putting pencil to paper, [and] the question I put to myself was shall I attempt to do something finer than the Choir or shall I content myself with merely carrying on the Choir design? The latter course was the easier and would save a lot of trouble and the result would be safe, though dull.

The alternative was a high aim, for to produce a Nave that was finer than the Choir was not a task that could be lightly tackled and I knew would involve difficulties in many directions, still I was confident and conceited enough to feel sure of achieving my object if I could get a free hand.

In arriving at a decision I felt sure that the right course was to aim high and not play for safety, for only in this spirit can fine work be done.

It is interesting and instructive to see what the mediaeval builders did in similar circumstances. Nearly all our Cathedrals were built in portions at different periods, so that we have numerous precedents to go by; these buildings also were designed by men who were natural artists and their work is the foundation and model for all Modern Gothic. Now what do we find? I know of no example where the later portions of a Cathedral or church imitated or continued the design of the earlier portion. It was the ambition of every builder to excel his predecessor and to do the finest work he was

capable of. Now the result to be noted is that instead of these Cathedrals etc. losing their toute ensemble effect by the variety of their parts, they positively gain by it, and when in rare cases, such as Salisbury, the whole building was erected at one period, the result was extremely dull and uninteresting. It might be argued that we do not want a Nave that is finer than the Choir, as the Choir should be the finest part of a church, but I do not think that this is the right view to take and it was certainly not the view taken by the mediaeval builders when they were faced with a similar proposition.[8]

In defending his ideas Scott was, of course, being disingenuous, for he must have known of the case of the nave of Westminster Abbey, for instance, where – a century and a half after the rebuilding began – Henry Yevele faithfully carried on the design of the eastern parts of the church. What this letter also suggests is that Scott did not share the reverence of the monks towards the work of Garner. That is not surprising; when obliged to work with G.F. Bodley after being given the commission for Liverpool Cathedral, Scott had found himself in uncomfortable conflict with the older and more conservative architect, who had been in partnership with Garner for three decades. Scott had also (in 1905) been asked to reconstruct Garner's Chapel of the Convent of the Visitation at Harrow after the recent building had become structurally unstable, and while he reused much of Garner's stonework he made the new chapel much more interesting and dramatic.[9] Although Scott was in the evolving tradition of the Gothic Revival and was much influenced by the earlier work of such architects as Bodley and Leonard Stokes – as well as by his father's churches and those of his master, Temple Moore – from the very beginning of his career, when he won the competition for Liverpool with his design for a 'Twentieth-Century Cathedral', he had demonstrated a desire to reinterpret Gothic with a modern and personal character.

All this, however, was of academic interest while the war continued, and even after the conflict ended in November 1918 there was no immediate prospect of building the nave until money could be raised. At the beginning of 1920, with insufficient funds secured, much-inflated post-war building costs and general economic and political instability, Butler was contemplating whether to build 'rather more than half the proposed nave, & close it in with a substantial brick wall, to last the next half century or so; or … [to] shorten the nave, finishing it off at the point the money runs out'.[10] Three months later, while not entirely abandoning hope of executing one of his first proposals, Scott sent drawings to illustrate a possible solution. This involved retaining the existing first bay of the nave (by Dunn and Hansom) and recognizing that, if the nave were to be a war memorial, it must be complete in itself. He wrote to Butler:

I have found the problem a difficult one because, owing to the great rise in prices, it would now only be possible to build the three additional bays of the nave, with the aisles, for £25,000, without allowing anything for a West front. A nave of only four bays would, it is true, provide sufficient seating accommodation, but it would be too short to make anything of architecturally, either inside or out, unless one could ultimately carry on the treatment in some way.

Scott then proposed an ingenious compromise:

Let us build the three new bays, thus completing the nave proper as a War Memorial, as desired; the West end being filled in with a temporary wall. Later, when funds permit, we can carry on the general treatment westward.

But this later section will not be the nave at all. It will consist of two stories, the lower one being a Narthex which, incidentally, can be used for additional seating without being in any sense part of the nave proper. The upper storey will be the Chapel … a fine effect would be produced by the raised chapel approached by the steps in the aisles; while the entry into the lofty nave through the comparatively low narthex could not fail to be very impressive.[11]

Fortunately, drawings for this, 'Scheme No. 3', survive and show how the high nave vaulting would have run continuously from the crossing into the western chapel, the floor of which was to be just above the level of the springing of the nave arcades. At the east end of this upper chapel, visible from below, was to be a tall, free-standing reredos rising dramatically above a semi-circular arch straddling the nave – a development of an idea that recurred in Scott's church designs, beginning with his early competition entry for Liverpool Cathedral. The monks were not impressed, however, while Butler questioned 'embarking on such a work in present disturbed state of everything. We shall probably wait until the Revolution is over.'[12]

By the end of the following year, however, Butler evidently felt the Revolution had passed, and, with building costs falling, he decided that work on the nave could begin. However, there was no hope of carrying out any of Scott's bold schemes: the monks were determined that the new nave should correspond with the eastern parts of the church and follow Garner's earlier conception for the nave, which, unlike his choir, was to have a triforium. Butler wrote to Scott, asking whether he was prepared to undertake something so conservative, explaining how

the Church belongs to the Community as a whole, & the building of the nave is a

The Gothic marriage
between Scott's nave and the
Dunn and Hansom transept.

community act, concerning which there has to be corporate agreement, at any rate of a large majority … [And] you will easily understand the fascination of Garner's name on the imagination & the judgement of most of our monks. I have to say that, after experimenting, the only line on which it is possible to secure any kind of general agreement is Garner's nave as first designed, i.e., with triforium. It is the same as the choir, except for the triforium. It is quite definitely the general wish that the nave be this.

Butler hoped Scott would think 'that Garner is a big enough figure, & you are a big enough figure in the architectural world, for you to be able to carry out his designs without any loss of prestige professionally'.[13]

Scott agreed to this restrictive brief. He was, however, concerned to harmonize with the earlier transepts by Dunn and Hansom as well as with Garner's choir. In January 1922 he wrote to the future Abbot, Bruno Hicks:

I understand that the Chapter are anxious to preserve a continuity of design with the existing work, and I think if this is the aim, it should be done thoroughly; and if a Triforium is desired (and with this I am in entire agreement), it should range as far as possible with the only part of the building that already contains a Triforium, namely the Transepts and the existing Nave bay; otherwise we should be introducing a third type of treatment into a building already containing two varieties … Garner also appreciated the value of only having two designs in the Church, as shown by his original scheme for the Nave and Choir. You will remember that my original designs for the Nave showed an entire departure from the Transepts and the Choir; but this was done in an endeavour to make the Nave finer … Now,

however, as continuity is to be our aim, I think the result would be far better attained by following the lines of Dun & Hanson's [sic] Triforium …, which gives a very good effect – finer, I think, than Garner's abandoned design.[14]

In May 1922 Scott was instructed to proceed with building seven (rather than five) new bays in addition to the existing nave bay, the mouldings and details of which were to be modified for consistency. His careful design ensured that the interior of the great church now seems a complete unity, harmonious throughout. The proportions, vaulting pattern and shafts of the choir were continued into the nave, as was the design of Garner's arcades (but with slightly simplified detail and less ornamental carving), while the design of Dunn and Hansom's triforium in the transepts was continued between the nave arcades and the wide clerestory windows above, filled with rather conventional Flowing Decorated Tracery. Only in the exterior treatment of the nave and in the southern chapels – placed, in common with Garner's further east, above the monks' cloister – does Scott's more distinctive and personal style of Gothic emerge, in such details as the stone railings and parapets. The treatment of the exterior of the north aisle is also distinctive, with buttresses combined with shafts and pinnacles.

The construction was carried out by the Abbey's own workmen under the supervision of Wilfred Collins, the resident clerk of works. The Bath stone was supplied by the Bath & Portland Stone Firms, Ltd, and the carving executed by Alfred B. Wall of Cheltenham. The nave, with its temporary west wall (two more bays were envisaged), was opened in July 1925. On that occasion, Scott was tactful, saying that 'he was sure that the Abbot and community had been right in insisting that the general lines of the existing building should be adhered to', but he surely regretted that his much bolder conception had not been carried out.[15]

The pity is, perhaps, that it is not immediately evident that the nave was intended as a war memorial. Abbot Leander Ramsay, who had succeeded Butler in 1922, suggested building on the north side of the nave a chantry chapel, similar to the Bubwith and Sugar chapels in Wells Cathedral, to make it clear, but Scott considered that 'the effect might be to mar the continuity of the arcade and to detract from the length and spaciousness of the nave as a whole'.[16] His solution, to place the names of the Fallen in a bay of the south aisle wall, was precluded by a ruling from Rome prohibiting the introduction in a church of names other than those of individuals buried therein. In the event, the names of the 110 Downside boys who had died in the war were placed on the base of a war memorial cross erected in 1925 in the Abbey grounds; those names were also carved into stone panels now fixed to the inside of Scott's temporary west wall.[17]

With a proper nave built at last, Scott's work at Downside was far from over; something had to be done about the furnishings of the eastern parts of the church. As James observed, with the new long vista, the 'faults [of the east end] proclaimed themselves more emphatically, the whole composition became more confused, its mistakes more patent' with 'the medley of beams and lamps[,] the distracting altar screens and the inadequate stall canopies to which it led the eye'.[18] Ramsay asked Ninian Comper to look at the problem, but his solution – to move the high altar to the west end of the choir – was too radical for the monks. Nothing was done until 1934, when Abbot Bruno Hicks asked Scott to consider the plan of the choir. At first he proposed a central altar with a ciborium above, but this, again, was not acceptable. In the event, Scott rearranged the sanctuary, and he did so with brilliant and effective economy, without significantly altering the existing floor levels (as Comper's scheme would have required).

A new high altar, 12 feet (3.7 m) wide and made from stones taken from the ruins of Glastonbury Abbey, was placed on three steps a little west of the existing altar, with a free-hanging tester above. Scott retained the stone screens to the north and south installed by Frederick Walters in 1907, but removed the three placed between Garner's piers at the east end of the choir. In their stead, Scott designed lower stone screens behind the eastern arcade, the outer ones running obliquely to connect with the smaller piers built on the foundations of the apse originally proposed by Dunn and Hansom. These screens both serve a purpose and provide a tangible memory of an earlier stage in the complicated, if comparatively short, history of the building: 'Sir Giles ... has reminded us that our church was planned at first with an apse ... Not only this, his screens give a new emphasis to the ambulatory, an emphasis that was needed.'[19]

With the long-standing problem of the choir resolved, the church could at last be consecrated. This took place on 12 September 1935. In the event, however, these sanctuary arrangements lasted for only three decades before Francis Pollen's reordering in 1968 at last moved the (shortened) high altar further west – as both Scott and Comper had recommended.

The choir also needed stalls. It had been Ramsay's desire to reproduce the medieval stalls of Chester Cathedral, and Abbot John Chapman, who succeeded him in 1929, was determined to carry out this project according to his wishes, although Ephrem Seddon suggested that stalls designed by Scott might be more successful. The stalls were made and carved, on the basis of measured drawings and photographs, by local workmen in the village of Ortisei in the Italian Tyrol, under the direction of the woodcarver Ferdinand Stüflesser. Scott was nevertheless instrumental in this curious project: not only was he very familiar with Chester Cathedral, having restored part of the fabric there, but also he had commissioned Stüflesser before the First World War (in what was then the Austrian Tyrol) to execute devotional carvings in several of his churches. And, with happy

RIGHT
Scott's original entrance to
the cloister from the nave.

OPPOSITE
The interior looking east.
Scott's paschal candle and
Easter frontal are shown
in situ.

symmetry, one of those was the new rood above the choir screen at Chester, installed in 1914 in place of the hanging cross designed by Scott's grandfather in the previous century. In the choir at Downside, modifications of the Chester model, the bishop's throne and additional woodwork were carried out to Scott's own design.

Other works by Scott inside Downside Abbey Church include the new screen to the organ in the south transept, put in place in 1931, and the funerary monuments of several former priors and abbots. These were the tombs of Abbots Ford and Ramsay and also that of Bishop Collingridge, Vicar Apostolic

of the Western District when the monks first came to Downside in 1814. The finest, however, is that erected for the prior who had begun the work of building the church, Cardinal Gasquet. For it, Scott proposed a recumbent effigy covered by a timber canopy to be placed under an arch in the south aisle of the choir. He took immense trouble with the commission, altering his first proposal in response to a request for 'richer treatment'.[20] The figure of Gasquet, in grey Palombino marble, was carved by Edward Carter Preston. 'I am sure you will like the work of the sculptor I have in mind,' Scott assured Chapman, 'as he is modern without being eccentric; he is a

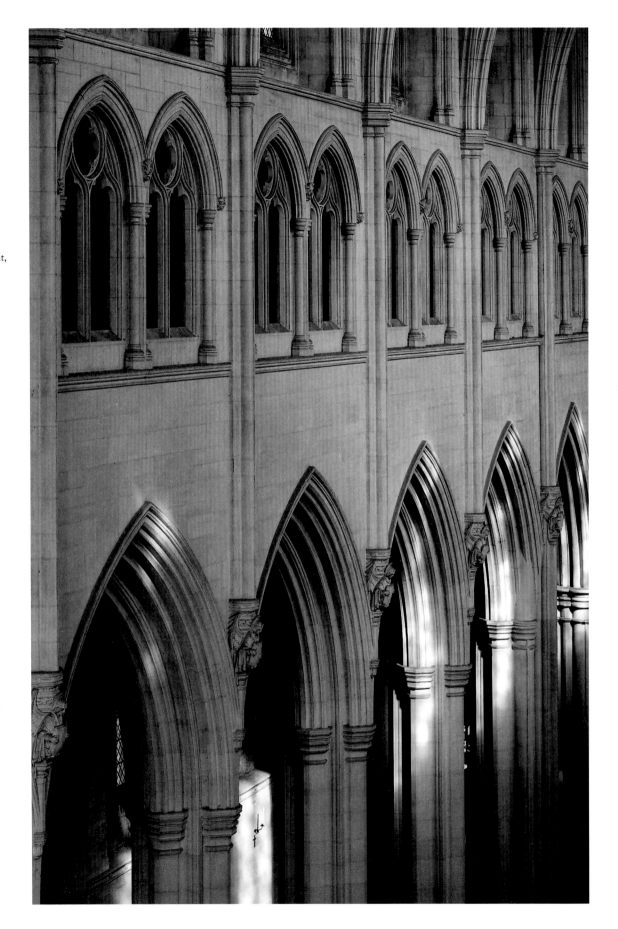

The nave, flooded with light, is unmistakably Scott, but its angels (with the names of St Gregory's superiors) provide continuity with Garner's choir.

The south aisle, looking west from Garner's choir to Scott's nave and the fifteenth-century statue of St Peter.

Liverpool sculptor, and I personally consider him a discovery.' When the Abbot hesitated at the price Carter Preston quoted (£700), Scott replied: 'I do not think this at all exceptional for a figure by a really good sculptor, which this man is; but of course the price of sculpture varies enormously and it would be possible to get a very much cheaper figure done by a commercial monumental sculptor, but this would not be worth having.'[21]

The canopy, of white pine, with its delicate Gothic detail, figures of saints on the eight piers and elaborate cresting with figures of angels, also required highly skilled work, and for this Scott was reluctant to employ Stüflesser's workshop: 'The price I have obtained is from Messrs Green & Vardy, of Islington, who would have the carving done by the same man who does my wood-carving for Liverpool Cathedral and who is, I consider, one of the finest Gothic carvers in the country.'[22]

Scott proposed that the woodwork be partially gilded, and even that required his close attention. When, alarmed by the estimate from Watts & Co., Chapman suggested the work could be done locally, Scott replied: 'I am afraid it is quite necessary to have the decoration done in London, as it is most important that I should be able to keep an eye on its progress. Moreover, the gilding done by the man I employ is a special process, arrived at after a very large amount of experimental work, and I myself do not know the secret of it.'[23]

The base of the effigy, of alabaster and dark reddish-brown Cornish marble, carved with an inscription, was supplied by the firm of W.H. Best, ecclesiastical sculptors of Cheltenham. The tomb was finally installed, tightly fitting between the arcade piers, in 1933. But even then Scott was not satisfied, for after inspecting it in person he 'decided that certain slight alterations to the decoration, etc., were necessary'.[24]

Scott regarded Gasquet's tomb as one of his best works, and it is certainly one of the finest examples of twentieth-century ecclesiastical art. He succeeded in giving a traditional medieval form, the tomb monument, a convincing modern interpretation, for the Gothic detail is typical of Scott and has a character that might almost be described as Art Deco. As with the work he undertook for Scott in Liverpool Cathedral, Carter Preston rose to the challenge magnificently with his formal and highly stylized effigy of the Cardinal lying with his head held by an angel, a figure of History at his feet and his hat placed on his legs. It is a superb work of modern sculpture – and very different in character and effect to another work installed in the church at about the same time.

The reredos in the chapel of St Sebastian, with a figure in alabaster of the suffering saint, commissioned by Ramsay from Comper, was completed in 1929 (see pp. 160–61). Scott visited Downside the following year. 'I took him to see the famous S. Sebastian's & the Lady Chapel Gates' (also by Comper), Hicks reported to Chapman. 'He admired the Reredos immensely – though he said it would be very much better in 100 years! and he liked the Gates also – but he had *no use* whatever for the statue which he described as irreligious[,] fleshy and inartistic. "Feeble" he called it, also … He certainly used terms about it exactly corresponding to my own opinions – so I was delighted.'[25]

Scott's final work at Downside involved improving the exterior of the church. In 1924 he had been asked whether flying buttresses should be added to the choir, for although no drawings or other evidence existed to confirm it, it was the oral tradition in the monastery that Garner had wanted them and that they were omitted on grounds of expense. Scott responded: 'Externally, the present clerestory wall of the choir is somewhat bald and dull in appearance, and I consider the addition of buttresses would be an improvement from the architectural point of view.'[26] Scott duly designed flying buttresses for the choir (there were none on his nave and he did not now propose adding any).

Scott's principal task, however, was to do something about Dunn and Hansom's unfinished Normandy steeple, which rose 132 feet (40 m) into the air. He had already impressed the monks with his pragmatic ability to make telling improvements, showing them, for instance (as James recorded), how Dunn and Hansom's Victorian Gothic windows on the monastery 'could quite easily be turned into good domestic Tudor ... Later on he did not shrink from drawing a picture of the tower with no further addition to it than an English battlemented top, as if to suggest that we need do no more to it than add a foot or two to give it a passably fine finish. Fortunately, when the time came, we were a little more ambitious.'[27]

Serious discussions about the tower began soon after the election of Abbot Chapman in 1929, when Scott proposed increasing the projection of Dunn and Hansom's buttresses 'so as to enlarge the silhouette ... I feel strongly that these buttresses should be given greater projection, to increase the apparent width of the tower, as I do not think a satisfactory result could be achieved by merely adding a top.'[28] The following year he wrote that 'I feel strongly that something ought to be done to the tower, and this would certainly be an enormous improvement, in spite of what some of the Fathers may think!' It seems that others had made suggestions for heightening the tower, for he wrote a few days later:

> The outline of this tower is very difficult to handle and it seems essential for the balance of the whole that it should come in a fair amount before reaching the battlemented top. Your scheme carries the tower up at the same width to the very top and the result would be an unsatisfactory outline, with a tendency to look wider at the top than at the bottom; that is the reason I got rid of the octagons before reaching the parapet ... I am afraid the

silhouette of a tower is a far more subtle question than most people imagine.[29]

By the careful use of batters and setbacks, Scott had already shown himself a master at designing elegant, powerful towers, such as those of his Northfleet church and William Booth College at Denmark Hill in London; and he would go on to create magnificent towers for the cathedrals at Liverpool and Oban and at Bankside Power Station in London (now Tate Modern).

The tower at Downside was at last altered and heightened in 1937–38, when its character was changed from French to English. Dunn and Hansom's coupled windows were cleverly reworked, their unsightly circular clock faces filled with

Model of the top part of Gasquet's effigy for Downside (1931–32) by Edward Carter Preston, in the University of Liverpool Art Gallery.

curvilinear tracery and their grand southern entrance at the base of the tower modified and completed, with three figures of saints placed in the tympanum (carved by R.L. Boulton & Sons of Cheltenham). Above the plain walling of Dunn and Hansom's severe structure rose a narrower tower with three tiers of coupled traceried openings below a battlemented top, framed by corner pinnacles. Its character is pure Somerset; indeed, in 1940 Scott posted back, with apologies for keeping it so long, 'the very interesting book on Somerset Church Towers, which was lent me from the Downside Abbey library some time ago when I was dealing with the completion of the tower'.[30] At nearly 166 feet (51 m) it is higher than any in the county other than the crossing tower of Wells Cathedral, and perhaps there is something slightly ungainly about it, as Scott's upper stages do not quite balance the rather brutal bulk below; but it is a masterly exercise in architectural pragmatism and a magnificent landmark from a distance.

Nikolaus Pevsner visited Downside Abbey Church in the mid-1950s and thought that 'with its commanding tower it is Pugin's dream of the future of English Catholicism at last come true'.[31] But then, as today, one element rendered that dream incomplete: the temporary west front to the nave. Scott had envisaged an additional two bays being built, and in 1938 he sent Hicks a design for the west end. This was a development of the west elevation he had produced in 1920 for his 'Scheme No. 3'. In this, a low, wide entrance arch leading to a narthex was placed under a single wide west window filled with an artful pattern of flowing tracery. The window Scott now proposed was very similar, but it extended further downwards, while the entrance arch below was much lower and led to a west door beyond the wide internal porch, which would have occupied the space below the gallery running across the westernmost bay.

'I felt rather pleased with the way it worked out,' Scott wrote to Hicks (who was about to step down),

and I think you would like it if you could see it in actual execution. With reference to your idea of a big central arch, I do not feel altogether in favour of this; I have tried it elsewhere and have not been entirely satisfied with the result. It always seems to have a rather unfortunate effect of breaking up the facade and destroying the unity which are [sic] very valuable in a composition of this kind; moreover, it rather tends to obstruct the detail of the West Window. It would, however, be quite easy to introduce more richness of detail, if this would meet your views.[32]

But such discussion was purely academic. The international situation was darkening, and the outbreak of another world war the following year put paid to any immediate prospects of replacing Scott's temporary brick wall with its triple simple lancet windows.

It was, perhaps, inevitable that Scott should be asked to design new buildings for Downside School in addition to working on the abbey church. The large scheme by Leonard Stokes designed before the First World War had been only partially carried out, and in 1929 Chapman asked Scott about a new art and science block. Scott responded by first considering the general layout for future expansion to 'give some coherence to the whole, which at present is sadly lacking'.[33] A new block was to balance Stokes's completed wing either side of an axis running south from the church tower. Stokes's tower would be mirrored by another tower and the two connected by a low single-storey wing. In the event, however, the new wing containing the science block and infirmary was placed closer to the Stokes building. The connecting wing was three storeys in height where it adjoined Stokes's tower, but only two further to the west because of the rise in the land, and Scott placed two additional 'squat towers' rising just above the roof – a feature that Sir George Oatley, architect of the

Cardinal Gasquet's hooded head supported by an angel, carved by Edward Carter Preston, Scott's principal sculptor at Liverpool Cathedral.

Scott's completion of the
Abbey tower is in homage to
Somerset church-building.

LEFT
The west front of the abbey church is connected directly to the monastic services building.

OVERLEAF
The unfinished west front is an austere facade, Cistercian in character.

huge Gothic Wills Memorial Building for Bristol University, considered adopting in his unexecuted schemes for enlarging the monastery.[34] The new buildings were faced in stone and designed in a severe abstracted Tudor manner; this harmonized with Stokes's architecture but also reflected the more modernistic style Scott was evolving for the secular and industrial commissions he was now tackling, such as Battersea Power Station in London.

The new science wing was completed in 1932. Six years later, Scott undertook his last commission for Downside when he began work on adding to Stokes's unfinished residential south range. Scott continued it eastwards to a satisfactory balancing termination, using Stokes's style and pattern of fenestration but cleverly incorporating a change in floor level necessitated by a new requirement for individual rooms for senior boys. This was completed in 1939. Yet again – as with the nave of the abbey

church – he managed successfully to make his work fit in harmoniously with the existing buildings, while introducing personal subtleties all of his own.

Finally, there was one further building designed by Scott for the monks of Downside, but it – like the converted barn at Midsomer Norton – was not on the abbey site. Nearby Bath had long had two churches for its Roman Catholic population, one of which, the Priory Church of St John the Evangelist, was served by the Benedictines of Downside. As the city expanded to the south, the Prior of St John's, Dom Anselm Rutherford, decided that a third place of worship was needed. A site was acquired in 1925 and Scott was asked to make a design. This was not Gothic, but Italianate. He was inspired by Rome, but not in the way that the architect John Wood had been two centuries earlier, for the suburb of Oldfield Park had nothing of the character of Georgian Bath. The new church, dedicated to St Alphege, was a simple

The abbey church and monastery stand above the Scott wing of the school, with Leonard Stokes's building on the right.

yet sophisticated essay in the round-arched manner fashionable for church architecture in the early decades of the twentieth century. The model, in both plan and style, was the Early Christian church of S. Maria in Cosmedin in Rome, and St Alphege's was built of rough Bath stone rather than smooth ashlar. The splendid baldachin of gilded oak, placed in a windowless apse, was again made by Stüflesser in Italy; the elaborate capitals were carved by W.D. Gough. The elaborately patterned floor, which resembles tessellated marble, is actually made of 'Ruboleum', a type of linoleum that Scott had proposed for the nave at Downside until funds enabled a stone floor to be laid.

Construction of St Alphege's began in 1927, and the first portion of the church was opened two years later. It was not consecrated until 1954 – two decades after the Benedictines had left Bath – and not completed until a few years later, unfortunately without the campanile Scott had designed. This church was, he later wrote, 'my first essay into the Romanesque style of architecture. It has always been one of my favourite works.'[35] 'I have at last seen the Church at Bath!', Chapman wrote to Scott shortly before it was blessed. 'I am delighted with it, as everyone else is. The baldacchino is very effective, and the pale blue in the pavement just prevents the whole from being too yellowy. The rough stone is a good colour."[36] In Giles Gilbert Scott the monks of Downside had found an accommodating architect who responded to their conservative tastes but who nevertheless created for them great works of modern architecture.

1. Scott to Butler, 26 April 1918.
2. Scott to Dom Ethelbert Horne, 20 November 1911; Butler to Dolan, 16 May 1912. Eternite was a cement-fibre material containing asbestos; Peter Howell (p. 45) notes that it was used for the Downside gymnasium in 1911.
3. Butler to Scott, 19 March 1913.
4. Scott to Butler, 2 January 1918; Butler to Scott, 5 January 1918.
5. Scott to Butler, 8 March 1918.
6. A. James, *The Story of Downside Abbey Church*, Stratton-on-the-Fosse, Somerset (Downside Abbey) 1961, p. 74. None of Scott's drawings survive at Downside, but a few of his early drawings, which indicate the character of the unexecuted schemes, are in the RIBA Drawings Collection.
7. *Ibid.*
8. Scott to Butler, 26 April 1918.
9. In the Downside Archives is a letter from R. Emily Garner, dated 22 July 1906, informing the abbot that 'Mr Bodley told me, that young Mr. Scott to whom the Harrow Chapel has been given, instead of having the defective bricks removed and replaced by sound ones, as he ought to have done, is making a new design!'
10. Butler to Scott, 7 January 1920.
11. Scott to Butler, 30 April 1920.
12. Annotation to a letter from John B. Lofting, Scott's surveyor, 31 August 1920.
13. Butler to Scott, 18 November 1921.
14. Scott to Hicks, 12 January 1922.
15. Quoted in James, *Story of Downside*, p. 77.
16. A.G. Crimp (of Scott's office) to Ramsay, 27 May 1924.
17. The war memorial in the grounds at Downside is mysterious in that no document or publication refers to its designer; Simon Johnson suggests that it was by Ephrem Seddon, who was responsible for the war memorial in Stratton-on-the-Fosse. The stone panels now placed on the inside of the temporary west end of the nave were commissioned in 1920 and at first fixed to the exterior of the earlier temporary west wall.
18. James, *Story of Downside*, p. 76.
19. *Ibid.*, p. 94.
20. Scott to Chapman, 19 February 1930.
21. Scott to Chapman, 28 August and 23 September 1931.
22. *Ibid.*
23. Scott to Chapman, 18 October 1932.
24. Scott to Chapman, 13 September 1933.
25. Hicks to Chapman, 12 February 1930.
26. Ramsay to Scott, 11 December 1924; Scott to Ramsay, 12 December 1924.
27. James, *Story of Downside*, p. 73.
28. Scott to Chapman, 11 June 1929.
29. Scott to Chapman, 5 and 10 September 1930.
30. Scott to Abbot Sigebert Trafford, 8 March 1940.
31. N. Pevsner, *North Somerset and Bristol*, London and Harmondsworth (Penguin) 1973, p. 183.
32. Scott to Hicks, 23 November 1938.
33. Scott to Chapman, 1 July 1929.
34. Chapman wrote to Scott on 4 September 1930:
    'I showed Sir G. Oatley today my latest plan [?] for the extension of the monastery, designed to be much cheaper than his. He is quite prepared to adopt them, even to two dumpy towers at the corners. But I told him it was *quite likely* I had got the idea of having these from your delightful design for our science block. Upon which he quite properly said that he could not imitate what you had done and that you might easily resent it. I said I should write and ask you if you would mind if what he draws has some (really accidental) likeness to your two dumpy towers. Imitation is the best part of flattery. But in this case he will never have actually seen your drawings.' Scott replied on 8 September that he had no objection: 'After all, squat towers are not my copyright, provided only the general idea and not the detail is reproduced.'
35. Quoted in Christopher Martin, *A Glimpse of Heaven: Catholic Churches of England and Wales* Swindon (English Heritage) 2006, p. 183.
36. Chapman to Scott, 28 June 1929.

The Work of Francis Pollen

Alan Powers

The work of two architectural firms dominated the post-war decades at Downside: Brett, Boyd and Bosanquet, followed by Brett and Pollen. There was a connection: Lionel Brett (1913–2004), later third Viscount Esher, dissolved the first practice and then, after an interval, went into partnership with Francis Pollen (1926–1987) from 1960 to 1970. In neither practice did Brett play a major design role, since his talents lay in city planning and working as a public figure for the architectural profession. Pollen, on the other hand, shunned publicity but possessed design ability of a rare order.[1] He came from a distinguished family of Catholic artists, beginning with his great-grandfather, John Hungerford Pollen (decorative painter, fellow of Merton College, Oxford, and Anglican priest in Leeds before his conversion in 1852), who, having lost his living and been disinherited by his rich uncle, married and became John Henry Newman's professor of fine arts in Dublin and designer of the University Church on St Stephen's Green.

Francis's father (Hungerford Pollen's grandson), Arthur Pollen, was a sculptor, and his mother another artist, Daphne Baring, whose painting as a student at the Slade School of Fine Art in London was much admired by the exacting head, Henry Tonks. Francis was aware from childhood of the work of Sir Edwin Lutyens, who converted Lambay Castle in Dublin Bay as a romantic retreat for Daphne's father, Cecil Baring, later Lord Revelstoke. After attending both Ampleforth and Downside during the Second World War, Francis studied architecture at Cambridge and at the Architectural Association in London. Initially, he resisted the post-war trend towards Modernism and was encouraged in this by Robert Lutyens, the architect son of Sir Edwin. Pollen's buildings of 1950–55 showed him to be an accomplished practitioner in a simplified version of the Lutyens manner, with a strong feeling for massive walls and the subtle placing of windows.

Around 1957 Pollen made a radical shift towards Modernism. While he objected to the spindly,

Through the work of Francis Pollen, Downside made a significant contribution to architecture in the 1960s. The library is in the foreground, with the monastic refectory and guest wing beyond.

insubstantial Modern style of the immediate post-war period, there were by this date examples of a heavier and more monumental treatment that may have given him the assurance he wanted that his love of massive structure could be incorporated into the Modern style. Le Corbusier's chapel of Notre-Dame-du-Haut at Ronchamp was completed in 1954, and his Dominican monastery of La Tourette in 1957, both buildings in which the expressive possibilities of concrete were demonstrated. In two small houses at Neuilly, the Maisons Jaoul (1950–55), Le Corbusier showed how massive brick could be combined with concrete columns and floor slabs to create an architectural language that had a considerable impact on British architecture, including the design of churches and of Pollen's first venture into the new style, the Lion Boys' Club in Pitfield Street, Hoxton, London (1958).

In 1952 the new, more monumental, hybrid of Modernism was emerging, and, for once, Britain was its centre. The movement acquired the name 'The New Brutalism', a term of complex origin; one of its meanings refers to the French term *béton brut*, which refers to the appearance of raw or untreated concrete when the shuttering into which it was poured is removed to reveal the marks of the timber. After a period when, owing to the exigencies of post-war shortages as much as any aesthetic factors, architects had often presented buildings with layers of cladding rather than revealing their underlying materials, the New Brutalists were committed to sober reality, but not without a self-consciousness about style. New Brutalist work was akin to the Gothic Revival and Arts and Crafts ways of building truthfully, revealing load-bearing structures and their joints but usually replacing timber with steel or concrete. The texture of materials was similarly valued, not to be covered up with such concealing finishes as plaster. It was, in many ways, an ideal style for monastic austerity. Along with a new ethical understanding about

honesty in building came a commitment to shaping society in a more honest and equitable manner.

A further but less self-evident aspect of New Brutalism was its recognition that Modern architecture did not entail a complete break with the past. It was, in many ways, a rather academic style, often based on the reinterpretation of underlying principles of historic buildings. Several of its British practitioners, including James Stirling and Peter and Alison Smithson, were inspired by the massive Baroque houses of John Vanbrugh (1664–1726), such as Seaton Delaval in Northumberland, and by the then dis-regarded London churches of Nicholas Hawksmoor (1661–1736). Pollen similarly brought sympathy with the past to his work, especially with Classical and Romanesque monuments in Greece and the more massive structures of ancient and medieval Italy that he saw on his way to and from national service in Palestine.

The publication in 1949 of *Architectural Principles in the Age of Humanism* by the German émigré art historian Rudolf Wittkower gave a different sort of insight into architectural history, one that – as the title suggests – was more an intellectual than a purely visual stimulus. It is hard to imagine that Pollen could not have read Wittkower's book, since it corresponds in so many ways to his designs for the library at Downside and the church at Worth Abbey (consecrated 1974; see p. 208) and was widely discussed among architects. Wittkower recovered the layers of meaning given to centralized building plans by Renaissance authors from Leon Battista Alberti onwards, as expressions of the divine perfection of the cosmos, writing:

With the Renaissance revival of the Greek mathematical interpretation of God and the world, and invigorated by the Christian belief that Man as the image of God embodied the harmonies of the Universe, the Vitruvian figure inscribed in a square and a circle became a symbol of the mathematical sympathy between microcosm and macrocosm. How could the relation of Man to God be better expressed, we feel now justified in asking, than by building the house of God in accordance with the fundamental geometry of square and circle?[2]

Dunn and Hansom had intended a library to form a western extension to the west wing of the monastery at Downside (where the short '*Diu Quidem*' wing stood), and plans by the Bristol firm Oatley & Lawrence in 1929 had followed that model. The renewal of the library as a building project in the 1960s was a natural sequel, spurred by the growth of both monastery and school in numbers, wealth and intellectual ambition, under Abbot Christopher Butler. Books were spilling over into cloisters and corridors. The librarian was Dom Mark Pontifex, but what would now be called the 'client representative' for the building project was Dom Philip (Anthony) Jebb, the brother of Pollen's former architectural partner, Philip Jebb, who was married to Pollen's sister Lucy. These connections go some way to explaining his selection as architect, but, aside from being an Old Gregorian, Pollen was by this time a partner in the firm of Brett and Pollen.

In a text about the library in *The Raven*, Pollen described how a scheme was prepared in 1962 for a building on this site, but 'owing to mixed feelings on the part of the monastic community and to the realisation that the main entrance to the Monastery should be on the east side as opposed to the west, this scheme was abandoned'.[3] From a notebook of Jebb's preserved in the Pollen collection of the Downside archives, it appears that he worked out the spatial requirements of the new library and at the same time specified some conditions for the site, notably that it should be a free-standing building (a precaution against fire) while connected to the monastery. It should be 'as compact and simple a building as possible', with no windows through which sunlight could endanger the books, and with room for

expansion to double the size. There was to be a public reading room, to which separate access was therefore needed from the outside.

Jebb then identified six possible sites to present to the community, including the '*Diu Quidem*' scheme of Dunn and Hansom. He favoured the 'East Wing' site, since he anticipated the completion of this wing 'to make a harmonious whole' that would also provide a point of public access to the monastery. Placing the library there would be less architecturally disruptive than the other options, and the expansion would be relatively easy if the library were extended to the north. When the matter was put to the vote at a chapter meeting on 20 December 1961, two other sites – the 'oblique angle behind Ball Place' and the 'Rose Garden' – were a close second and third, but it was agreed by eighteen votes to thirteen to proceed with plans for the East Wing site. Pollen's narrative continues: 'We were asked to design a building on the present site in conjunction with a new design to replace the temporary East Wing of the Monastery'.[4]

Jebb's notebook includes a number of sketch plans in his own hand. These begin as rectangular plan forms, with librarians' rooms and catalogue space close to the entrance, and the reading room and book stacks beyond. In the verbal specification that follows, a design begins to take shape in three dimensions, with the idea of a 14-foot-high (4.3 m) reading room divided by a mezzanine, in which intimate study areas could be inserted beneath the low ceiling, flanked by bookshelves but looking out into the taller space. Only one page afterwards there is a rough drawing of a circular building with a central core and rooms radiating from it, clearly the germ of the library as built. This is developed with more precision in the pages that follow, with a scale plan and a section. No other documents have survived in the monastery papers or among Pollen's archives to prove whether Jebb was the hidden hand in the design, or whether Pollen was already involved in discussions with him. The high level of

OVERLEAF
Francis Pollen's refectory and guest wing block stitched the Victorian buildings together with reticence but not without architectural character of its own. His elevations are modelled to provide contrasts of light and shadow.

architectural understanding in the previous pages of the book suggests that Jebb could well have arrived at this solution single-handed, and although he can no longer recall with certainty that this was the case, he believes it was likely, given his interest in his brother's professional work.

In the notebook, the centrally planned library started as a circle and then, as in the finished building, became an octagon on a square base, with its angles facing the cardinal axes. This feature is found in the completed building, and adds movement and interest that would have been lacking had the faces of the octagon simply been aligned with the square base. It was a subtle but crucial design decision that helps to establish an identification between the library and the apse of the Lady chapel, with its typical polygonal Gothic plan, which looms over it on the northern side. The back cover of the notebook provides a final clue, with a diagram of two squares rotated on a circle to make the octagon form, a diagram remarkably like some engravings on the same theme illustrated by Wittkower from Bartoli's edition of Alberti's *De Re Aedificatoria*, 1550.[5] A later single sheet shows a three-dimensional drawing of the constituent volumes. Again, while the hand is Jebb's, it may be that the concept was Pollen's. Either way, it seems to have been an unusually fruitful collaboration. Pollen's first set of drawings, dating from 1963, show a twelve-sided figure that would have been too close to a circle and consequently less powerful; it was quickly abandoned.

The volume of the building is contained within an imaginary 60-foot (18.3-m) cube. The central core is a shaft for a book lift, around which is wrapped a spiral stair in its own concrete cylinder. The spaces at each level are threaded on this core, appearing outwardly like a series of nuts assembled on a bolt. The base, containing basement and ground-floor levels of book stacks, is square on plan. The external walls are faced in ashlar with unequal coursing that gives

emphasis to the horizontal lines. The face of these walls is 'battered' inwards in a pronounced way, a typical feature of Pollen's designs, giving a sense of strength under compression. The next level is a ring of dark engineering brick, facing the concrete construction behind. It has the appearance of a 'washer' in the nut-and-bolt assemblage, and makes a transition between the square base and the octagonal forms above.

The first of these is a narrow band of windows lighting the level containing offices, the catalogue room and a small lecture room. Above this, the main body of the library is expressed in double panels of obscured glazing held in simple iron frames, painted dark brown. Inside, there are two levels of shelving, the upper being a mezzanine gallery and the lower containing study carrels between the shelving units. Eight white cylindrical columns rise from floor to ceiling, standing free between the mezzanine and the perimeter glazing. On the level below, the columns are closer to the edge and connected to the wall, although there is space for the glazing to pass outside them. The columns contain hidden rainwater pipes. In the library, the glass is a striking feature, since it admits light but prevents any sort of view out. Pollen explained: 'The full-height glazing to this room consists of an outer sheet of tinted heat-absorbing glass, an inner sheet of plain glass and an interlay of white fibreglass. This has the triple effect of reducing solar heat gain in summer, internal heat loss in winter and effectively cuts out direct sunlight which would eventually destroy the bindings. The translucent effect of the fibreglass provides a high level of soft diffused light for reading.'[6] An incidental benefit of these windows, no doubt intended, was their reflection of the Gothic church, the trees and the sky.

The final level of the building is a windowless special collections library, with a wall of bush-hammered concrete, set well back to match the shape of the mezzanine beneath. The lift machinery needed to project above the roof, and required an appropriate

The library is composed in the manner of nuts and washers threaded on to a bolt, giving an impression of strength and power. The tall windows of the library are deliberately opaque, and from the outside offer reflections of the abbey church.

architectural housing. A glazed tent shape was proposed at one time, but the final form is more dynamic: a triangular shape like the gnomon of a sundial, angled towards the abbey church, suggesting perhaps a wing-nut holding everything down, the rotating cowl of an oast house or even a rocket launcher. At La Tourette, Le Corbusier introduced a number of such angular rooftop forms, although nothing quite like this. The waterspouts projecting in the manner of concrete gargoyles from the top level of the library are a more direct borrowing from Le Corbusier's prototypes, popular at the time among British designers.

Bush-hammered concrete was not part of Le Corbusier's repertoire, but it became popular among British architects in the 1960s. The concrete is cast with projecting ribs, usually vertical, which are then partially broken away with a pneumatic hammer to create the contrast of rough texture standing proud of a smooth background. This catches the light and also avoids the inevitable streaking of fair-faced concrete by the action of weather. It was in use by engineers on bridges before the Second World War, but came to prominence in the Elephant and Rhino Pavilion at London Zoo by Hugh Casson and Neville Conder, completed in 1965, where it was used as an analogy with the animals' crumpled hide.

In common with other Pollen designs, the library has some of the quality of a military building, whether Martello tower or Castel Sant'Angelo. This quality is conveyed not only by the overall form, but also by the slit windows between the book stacks in the base and the blind glazing of the main library. Despite its evident solidity, the shape of the library could also be interpreted as an object prepared for launching into the sky, or perhaps one that has just descended. This may sound fanciful, but Pollen was moved when, not long before his death, he watched the film *Close Encounters of the Third Kind*, with its hovering mother ship, which he was willing to see as an analogy to the abbey church at Worth.

The construction of the library was unusual, since it was built – as earlier Downside projects – entirely under the direction of the Downside clerk of works, Charles Howard, with his own team of eight men. Pollen wrote: 'This building is inevitably complex and produced some severe constructional problems for Mr Howard. To myself and to all those concerned with the building, he has proved that his competence and quality of workmanship are more than equal to that of any commercial firm.'[7]

While most building contracts require maximum speed as an aspect of economy, the priority at Downside was reversed, and the building rose gradually, one level at a time, as recorded in photographs by Jebb preserved in two albums with dates and other annotations. The foundations were excavated at the beginning of 1965. During 1966 the structure began to emerge above ground level, and at the beginning of 1967 the stairwell was rising to second-floor height. The photographs have a personal and quasi-medieval quality, with trial full-size layouts of the octagonal shapes on the grass and an apprentice spearing corks that had fallen down into the shuttering, prior to the pouring of the concrete. The octagonal library took shape during 1968, and the major construction continued into 1969, with the 'sundial' cast in October. In March 1970 the windows were installed, followed by the bookshelves and other furnishings, which were simply but finely made, some of them wedge-shaped to suit the form of the building.

The outline of a future library extension was included on some of the plans as an L-shape to the east and north of the existing library, but no other information about its form is available. Given that the present library has become overcrowded with books and archives, it would be a project worth reviving. Pollen also made a design for steps leading down to the link and the monastery entrance; it would have organized the spaces round the library into a more fitting approach than the present, rather unplanned descent of the slope.

The group of Pollen's
buildings created new external
spaces that were intended
to receive a more considered
landscape design treatment,
including terraces and steps.

In 1964 Pollen began work on the design of a new church at Worth Abbey in West Sussex (a daughter house of Downside), a scheme that ran in parallel with the library at Downside. In his Worth design, Pollen was able to synthesize the influences of Lutyens and Modernism with a force that grew out of the basic forms and materials chosen. The decision to adopt a centralized plan, in accordance with the Second Vatican Council, set the architectural problem of reconciling a square base with a circular super-structure, which Pollen solved with structural daring and formal finesse. The relationship between the square and the circle was also the basic design proposition of the Downside library, although the buildings differ in most other respects.

When the Downside library was finished, the building team moved on to build the new monks' refec-tory, with a school refectory below and guest rooms over it. It replaced a temporary building, known as the White House, constructed on the terrace over the unfinished Weld cloister (a lower-level building linking school and monastery at the west end of the main refectory, and lacking a vault). Here brick plays a major role; concrete is used for massive exposed beams resting on concrete pads over the brick piers between the windows. The design, arrived at after several variants, is based on a system of repeating bays, in line with the older buildings of the monastery. The refectories are given broad windows, above which the elevation design changes, via a jettied projection supported by the roof beams of the refectory. The guest rooms, of which there were originally intended to be two storeys, have projec-ting bay windows with two sides finishing in a sharp angle, another Gothic reference that also produces an attractive internal space, and the possibility of opening either window depending on wind direction. The upward continuation would certainly have made a better effect for this building, although with its omission some eastward views from the older part of the monastery were left uninterrupted.

This east wing also houses a bursary and what is now a development office, and provides, as intended, a point of public access to the monastic complex. School pupils pass along the lower corridor (the Weld cloister) and ascend a magnificent flight of steps designed by Pollen on their way to church. The stairwell is top-lit, and the light washes down the sandy-coloured bricks, which are flush-pointed in the manner of Lutyens, as are the walls of the refectory and the other structural wall surfaces of the east wing. The refectory ceiling between the beams is made of polished hardwood with ribs, angled down towards the centre, folded to correspond to the angles of the window heads. The glazing at the upper level of the T-shaped windows wraps over the brick walls and thereby clearly shows how the beams 'travel' through from inside to outside. This was standard for many buildings of the period.

The size and weight of these beams was a test for the crane available on site. The one at the point where the cloister leading to the church makes a sidestep was exceptionally long, and although it was cast in one piece, it was necessary to cut it and lift it in two parts. For this purpose, the main crane was used to lift a smaller crane on to the roof of the unfinished building, thoroughly supported by Acrow props at every level. The small crane was then used to raise and position the two halves of the beam.

The link between the library and the east wing was always part of the scheme, but was left until both were finished. There is a more elaborate design (of 31 July 1964) by Pollen in the archives, with hollowed-out niches to contain windows. These bear on the piers below with a flared head supported on a small point of contact, an arrangement similar to that of the columns in the church at Worth, but more exaggerated in the contrast of strength and fragility. When it came to construction, the design was greatly simplified, with rusticated stone piers and a much plainer corridor above, in character with Pollen's

classroom block (*c.* 1968; to the south of the church), which in turn derived its walling from the work of Leonard Stokes. The classrooms were Pollen's only contribution to the school buildings, and a notable one, now altered by an additional upper storey and enclosed escape staircase, but not overwhelmed by these changes.

In the abbey church, Pollen was commissioned in 1968 to make major changes to the high altar, fulfilling an intention expressed before the war by Ninian Comper to move the altar further west, although with a simplicity that Comper would not have condoned. The new sanctuary allows a clear view to the monks' choir and its elaborately carved stalls (lit by Pollen's own design of light-fitting, made from sections of plastic rainwater pipes). The sanctuary is flanked by two pairs of low stone walls, heavily battered in Pollen's preferred manner.

Pollen's other contribution to the community was to design a church in 1970 for the nearby village of Chilcompton, one of Downside's dependent parishes. In contrast to the monastery buildings, he was working here to a very tight budget, but by using a simple shallow-pitched roof with overhanging eaves and white-painted brickwork with round-arched windows and doors, he was able to add charm and character while making the most of the fine view. The steep hillside seems an apt setting for what appears similar to a southern European wayside chapel.

Pollen rarely worked in close proximity to pre-Modernist buildings, and Downside reveals his achievement in creating a dialogue with them. It was a problem that faced Modernist architects working in Oxford and Cambridge colleges at the end of the 1950s, such as Powell & Moya at Christ Church and Brasenose, and Architects' Co-Partnership at St John's, Oxford. They shifted from the lightweight look of the early 1950s to use stone and concrete together, and in the process developed a vocabulary of detail that was new to British architecture, with conscious reference to the language of load and support found in traditional construction, modified with a Mannerist play of form involving complex geometrical transitions and junctions. The source for this complex, introverted phase of Modernism could be traced to post-war Italian architecture, represented by such designers as Ernesto Rogers, Ignazio Gardella and Carlo Scarpa. As with sixteenth-century Italian Mannerism, which was simultaneously rediscovered by art historians and widely popularized, these architects took an existing style that was identified as pure and subverted it in order to enrich and sustain its communicative function. This was a move cognate with New Brutalism, and evident in the work of Peter and Alison Smithson in the 1960s in such designs as the Economist Plaza in St James's, London, or the Garden Building at St Hilda's, Oxford, or in the highly sculptural designs of Howell, Killick, Partridge & Amis.

The Downside library and its associated buildings can be seen in this light as representatives of a tendency in post-war architecture too readily misunderstood as simply a continuation of an earlier Modernist programme adapted to historical contexts. It is, in fact, more richly loaded with contradiction and symbolic meaning expressed through the essence of the structure and design.

The monastic refectory inverts the usual form of timber ceiling, which here slopes down towards the middle, giving added contrast of form and material as well as catching the light and reducing the visual weight of the beams.

1. On Pollen's life and work, see A. Powers, *Francis Pollen, Architect 1926–1987*, Oxford (Robert Dugdale) 1999. The account in that volume of the work at Downside was written without recourse to the monastery archives, and the present essay should be taken to supersede it. I am grateful to Dom Aidan Bellenger and Dr Simon Johnson for their help and hospitality at Downside, and to the members of the community who gave me their recollections, especially Dom Philip Jebb.

2. R. Wittkower, *Architectural Principles in the Age of Humanism*, London (Academy Editions) 1973, p. 16.

3. *The Raven* 62 (1971), pp. 18–19.

4. *Ibid.*

5. Wittkower, *Architectural Principles*, p. 16.

6. *Op. cit.* n. 3.

7. *Ibid.*

Index

This book's completion owes more to Dr Simon Johnson than to anyone else. His editorial work, dedication and patience throughout have been exemplary. Help has been provided also by Dr Stella Fletcher and by many members of the Downside monastic community, including Dom Michael Clothier, Dom Charles Fitzgerald-Lombard, Dom James Hood, Dom Philip Jebb and Dom Benet Watt. Paul Barker's wonderful photographs, which so enhance this book, gave the opportunity to explore many parts of the building.

Dom Aidan Bellenger
Twelfth Abbot of Downside

AMY FROST is Curator of Beckford's Tower and Museum in Bath, Collections Manager of the Bath Preservation Trust and a regular guest lecturer in the department of Architecture and Civil Engineering of the University of Bath.

MICHAEL HALL has published several books on nineteenth-century architecture and design, including *The Victorian Country House* (2009). He is completing a book on G.F. Bodley and Thomas Garner.

PETER HOWELL was educated at Downside School (1954–58) and at Balliol College, Oxford. He taught Classics in the University of London (Bedford and Royal Holloway Colleges) for thirty-five years. He is a former chairman of the Victorian Society.

RODERICK O'DONNELL has been writing about Downside and the Catholic Gothic Revival for thirty years. Since 1982 he has been an Inspector with English Heritage (and of Crown Buildings since 2004), and he was elected Fellow of the Society of Antiquaries in 1999.

ALAN POWERS is Professor of Architecture and Cultural History at the University of Greenwich. He has written a monograph on Francis Pollen (1999) and a number of other books on twentieth-century British architecture, including *Modern: The Modern Movement in Britain* (Merrell, 2005) and *Modern Architectures in History: Britain* (2007).

GAVIN STAMP, Hon. FRIAS, Hon. FRIBA, FSA, is an architectural historian with a long-standing interest in the Gilbert Scott dynasty, among other architects. He has written elsewhere about Giles Gilbert Scott's churches, power stations, House of Commons and telephone boxes.

First published 2011 by

Merrell Publishers Limited
81 Southwark Street
London SE1 0HX

merrellpublishers.com

British Library Cataloguing-in-Publication data:
Downside Abbey : an architectural history.
1. Downside Abbey (Bath, England) 2. Downside
Abbey (Bath, England) – History.
I. Bellenger, Dominic Aidan.
726.7'71'0942383-dc22

ISBN 978-1-8589-4542-2

Produced by Merrell Publishers Limited
Designed by Alexandre Coco
Project-managed by Rosanna Lewis
Proof-read by Barbara Roby
Indexed by Vicki Robinson

Printed and bound in China

*Unless otherwise noted, all quoted letters are in the
Downside Abbey Archives.*

Jacket, front: Cardinal Gasquet with angel, carved by
Edward Carter Preston; see p. 192.
Jacket, back: The abbey church from the south-east.

Page 2: The day comes to a close as the tower glows
among the trees.
Page 6: The north transept with Dunn and Hansom's
rose window.
Pages 10–11: The abbey church commands the local
countryside, the colour of its stones complemented
by the trees.
Page 216: The elongated windows and the buttresses
of Garner's choir, the stately tower, the copper roof of
the Lady chapel, the High Victorian Petre cloister
and the Modernist additions are all evident in this
characteristic view from the south.
Page 222: St Benedict, patriarch of the monks,
contemplates his Rule.